Guide to Transforming Teaching Through Self-Inquiry

Guide to Transforming Teaching Through Self-Inquiry

by

James Pelech
Benedictine University

Information Age Publishing, Inc.
Charlotte, North Carolina • www.infoagepub.com

Library of Congress Cataloging-in-Publication Data

CIP data for this book can be found on the Library of Congress website
http://www.loc.gov/index.html

Paperback: 978-1-62396-159-6
Hardcover: 978-1-62396-160-2
E-Book: 978-1-62396-161-9

Printed in the United States of America

CONTENTS

PREFACE

As best as I can remember, this book has been developing for well over 30 years, though not always as a conscious endeavor. Even as a young teacher I reflected upon my work, though many of these attempts were haphazard. As a young teacher I would become frustrated because, despite my attempts at reflecting on and improving my practice, I did not have a systematic way of doing so. And that is the point of this book—to provide a visible, concrete, cohesive, and unified system of teacher self-inquiry. Many of the ideas presented here are ideas or practices you and I have already tried. My purpose is to organize these practices into a system that is connected and is supported by sound educational theory and educational research. This brings up a critical point: I did not want to just present a book filled with "how to" procedures or recipes; and so, in this book I use research and accepted theory to provide a foundation that supports the presented practices.

Using authentic situations to drive instruction is a passion of mine, and that is why you will see in this book examples of actual hand-written journal entries and notes. In some cases I have changed a few words and sentences to ensure readability; in other cases I have borrowed bits from different authentic cases and pieced them together in order to present a situation that is clear and concise. Overall, however, I have tried to present as authentic a book as possible.

In writing this book I have had many enjoyable experiences, and I learned a great deal about teacher self-inquiry. I hope you will, too. Enjoy!

Guide to Transforming Teaching Through Self-Inquiry, p. ix
Copyright © 2013 by Information Age Publishing
All rights of reproduction in any form reserved.

ACKNOWLEDGMENTS

As always, I must first thank my wife, Gwen, for being a wife beyond compare. No matter what goal I am pursuing, she is there for me. She does a great job of blending the roles of advocate, coach, cheerleader, mentor, and best friend; the best part is that she mixes these roles effortlessly and sprinkles them with genuine love. Gwen has been the inspiration for pursuing my doctorate and for my two books, especially this one. There were many days when I wondered whether I could complete this project, but she always seemed to know how to say the right words at the right time.

My son, Chris, not only has been a pleasure to parent, but he has been a motivating force. Watching Chris grow and mature as a person and as a student has provided great inspiration for me. His modeling of energy and determination has been a huge influence. As I have said before: Chris, the best is yet to come.

My best friend, Rich Shewmake, is a living model of what it means to be a true friend. Whether it has been working together as educators or being a fan at the games I was coaching, or encouraging me while I worked on my doctorate, Rich has been there and has been steadfast in his support. Well, Rich, it looks like we have gone through another "excellent adventure."

Dr. Gail Pieper, my editor, has been a true ally. Her professional advice has been invaluable, and there is no price to put on the encouragement she has provided. She has made the writing of my two books a great experience.

Dr. Alan Gorr, my dean, is to be recognized for his continual mentoring and coaching. He has always made time for me and has demonstrated

Guide to Transforming Teaching Through Self-Inquiry, pp. xi–xii
Copyright © 2013 by Information Age Publishing
All rights of reproduction in any form reserved.

a great deal of patience guiding my transition from high school teacher to college professor. I cannot thank him enough.

Dr. MeShelda Jackson, my department chair, has truly supported me in all my endeavors. I must mention her great sense of humor—she is one of the few people who really "gets my jokes." Thanks, MeShelda.

My teaching colleagues in the School of Education at Benedictine University deserve a big "thank you" for their personal and professional friendship. I feel extremely fortunate to work with such people, and I want them to know that.

Mrs. Sally Shore of Benedictine University has been a tremendous friend and supporter. She deserves to be recognized for her help on the diagrams and pictures, and she has been a calming influence on me.

The friendship, support, and camaraderie provided by Mrs. Joyce Cecchi have been priceless. Working with such a professional who is also a genuine person has been a real blessing. Everyone should have the privilege of working with such a nice person.

A special recognition must go to Mrs. Denise Spells and Mrs. Lillie Pass of Saint Ethelreda School. I have had the privilege of working with these two people through our university partnership for 7 years. They have truly demonstrated what it means to be real educators. I want them to know how much I admire and appreciate them.

A special "thank you" goes to Mr. George Johnson, founder and publisher of Information Age Publishing. I thank George for believing in me and for providing the opportunity to have my work published.

And of course, I must thank all the students whom I have had the pleasure of working with over the years. They are the reason I have enjoyed teaching so much. It is their enthusiasm, curiosity, and trust in me which has enabled me to "rock and roll" in the classroom. It is because of my students that I cannot wait for the next 40 years of teaching.

CHAPTER 1

INTRODUCTION

We provide here a sneak preview of the ideas contained in this book. These ideas will help you, the educator, transform your teaching in order to improve student learning. This book contains both theory and practice; we view these two not as separate but as complementing each other.

This idea is not new. In rejecting the notion that theory and practice are distinct entities, Cole and Knowles (2000) write that "practice and practical action are recognized as an embodiment and expression of theory, and teachers are, by extension, recognized as theory builders" (p. 10). Argyris and Schön (1974) remind us that all people—including professional practitioners—"must become competent in taking action and simultaneously reflecting on this action to learn from it" (p. 4). The creation of knowledge, the application of this knowledge into action, and reflection on the effectiveness of this action require a certain type of thinking. Since teaching is done in an ever-fluctuating environment, a teacher must continually recreate frames of mind, question previous underlying assumptions, formulate new mental frames of reference, and devise new meaning schemes. Mezirow (1991) refers to this process as "transformative learning." It is the analysis of a teacher's everyday actions and personal theories by the reframing of meaning schemes, frames of reference, and underlying assumptions that leads to the transformation of one's teaching. Such self-inquiry clearly involves a great deal more than merely describing classroom practices and teacher behaviors; it requires analyzing and creating plans to modify or change current assumptions and philosophical foundations framing one's practice.

Guide to Transforming Teaching Through Self-Inquiry, pp. 1–6
Copyright © 2013 by Information Age Publishing
1

1.1 Teacher Self-Inquiry

Just exactly what does teacher self-inquiry involve? What platforms deliver teacher self-inquiry? In this section we look at examples of teacher self-inquiry and examine how they contribute to the transformation of teaching. Each example is followed by a brief analysis. Many more examples will be examined in subsequent chapters.

Example 1: Journal Entry

The first example comes from a journal entry from one of my college classes on assessment. In this class, as well as my other classes, I deliver course content using a Constructivist, student-centered philosophy. A deep conviction of mine is that I should model for my students what I want them to do as teachers. I believe that those in a leadership position, such as teachers, should "practice what they preach." Additionally, I feel that my courses should be as practical as possible; this conviction stems from many years of hearing my high-school math students ask, "When are we going to use this stuff?" The following journal entry explains this conviction—and the resulting dilemma. This handwritten note (Figure 1.1) is actually a recopying of the original note; the recopying was done for legibility reasons and for a few minor grammatical modifications.

Analysis: This journal entry is more than a recall of class events; it is the recognition that certain class activities conflict with my philosophical foundations. This recognition is the beginning of the transformation process. Transformation begins when a present situation does not align with one's philosophical perspective or assumptions. While this journal entry does not present an action plan for the transformation process, it is the trigger for this process.

The second example comes from my tenure portfolio. Like the journal, a portfolio can help transform one's teaching practice. Each artifact has a "rationale" that aligns with it and can be used as a self-inquiry tool to examine the artifact. Figure 1.2 is an example.

Analysis: Like the previous example of self-inquiry, the rationale is more than a mere description of teaching activities. It examines why the artifact is meaningful, and it projects a plan of how it will influence future teaching. These are the foundations of true teacher self-inquiry. In this case the value of the artifact stems from the fact it represents the philosophical foundation of modeling the Constructivist philosophy. Additionally, it represents transformation by presenting a possible approach for integrating collaboration into teacher education.

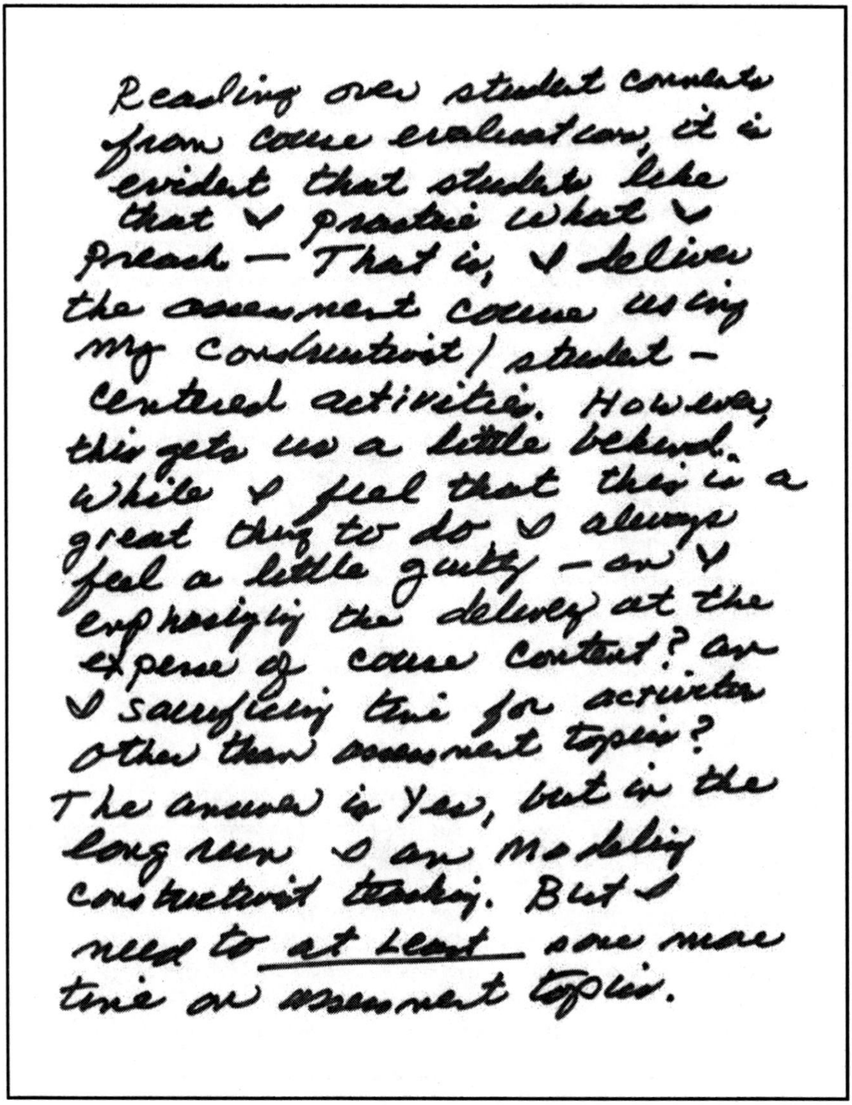
Reading over student comments
from course evaluations, it is
evident that students like
that I practice what I
preach — That is, I deliver
the assessment course using
my constructivist/student-
centered activities. However,
this gets us a little behind.
While I feel that this is a
great thing to do, I always
feel a little guilty — am I
emphasizing the delivery at the
expense of course content? am
I sacrificing time for activities
other than assessment topics?
The answer is Yes, but in the
long run I am modeling
constructivist teaching. But I
need to at least some more
time on assessment topics.

Figure 1.1. Sample journal entry.

The third example comes from an interactive journal, in which a person writes some comments (perhaps in response to a question or "prompt") and a colleague responds to the journal entry. This interaction can be between colleagues, between a teacher and a coach, or between teacher and student. Figure 1.3 is a student's response to a prompt I gave in a methods class, with Figure 1.4 showing my own response.

Title of artifact: Cross–Curricular Project

What the artifact is: This artifact describes a cross-curricular project that my Middle/High School Math Methods class participated in with Dr. Wong and his Middle/High School Science Methods class. The purpose of this activity was to have students in both classes create and implement a secondary/middle school-level class using the domains of science and math. This artifact has four components. The first component is a document examining the importance of the cross-curricular approach in education, especially education for pre-service teachers. The second component is a packet that presents the components of this project. The third component is a copy of the results of the survey students filled out. The fourth component is a reflection on this artifact.

Why the artifact is important: This artifact is important because it demonstrates the ability to make curricular adjustments to help prepare pre-service teachers for teaching in the twenty-first century. This Cross-Curricular Project is an example of modeling and implementing the Constructivist philosophy. The hallmark of interaction enters into this artifact; math methods students interact and collaborate with science methods students. Student comments indicated that they realized that collaboration is a complex, multidiscipline process that must be studied in order to be implemented.

Another important aspect of this artifact is that it involved interaction between students and instructor. The results of the survey served as an instrument for a rich class discussion.

What I learned doing the artifact: The implementation of cross-curricular teaching is a multifaceted endeavor. This includes, but is not limited to, different vocabularies and different frame of minds for different content areas.

What I will do in the future: In collaboration with Dr. Wong, I will be working on analyzing the results of the survey, and writing an article on this project. I also plan to work with Dr. Wong on extending this project into both of our Middle/High School methods courses. Also, I will work on developing a framework for structuring the art and science of collaboration. Collaboration must be presented to students as an entity formed by cognitive science and sociological principles.

Figure 1.2.   Sample portfolio entry.

Analysis: The student journal entry indicates that the student has begun the process of building a philosophical foundation for his practice. In this case the student identifies the purpose of teaching as that of helping students. The instructor's response seeks to extend this. The response does more than recap what was said—it encourages the student to turn his ideas into concrete action.

Prompt

What have we done, that has changed why you want to teach?

Answer

I think the more stories that I hear about a teacher helping a student in need makes me want to teach even more. Without teaching there is no way to know what the students will confront you with. I think it will be an awesome thing to do to help a student in need, or have a positive effect on their life. I realize now more then ever how many students are in need of a positive role model and I want to be that person for them.

Figure 1.3. Student response to prompt.

You hit on the essence of teaching and that is of helping students; while the content is important the be-all and end-all of teaching is that of helping students → it really is it really is a "people business." So, here is my challenge: What is your plan for developing your helping skills? In other words, how will you use your course work to improve your helping skills?

Figure 1.4. Teacher response.

1.2 Summary

This chapter has previewed some of the ideas, concepts, and platforms presented in the rest of this book. You've had a glimpse of a few of the tools used for transforming teaching through self-inquiry. The subsequent chapters of this book not only present and examine the foundations for such a system; they provide the mechanics and examples of such a system.

CHAPTER 2

WHAT DO TEACHERS DO?

As seen in Chapter 1, reflection is an important aspect of what teachers do when they teach. This chapter examines reflection in more detail. Before we do so, however, let us look at an overarching question. Since the aim of education, and thus of teaching, is to help students learn, we need to examine what really affects student learning the most. How does the teacher fit into such an examination? How important is the teacher? How important is teacher reflection?

2.1 Teacher Effects on Learning

The initiative to examine the importance of the teacher was given a large push in 1998 with the reauthorization of Title II of the Higher Education Act, which requires the Secretary of Education to issue annual reports concerning teacher quality across the nation. A U.S. Department of Education report (2003) states the existence of "consistent evidence that individual teachers contribute to student achievement" (p. 2). Let us take a look at specific studies that confirm this statement.

Wright, Horn, and Sanders (1997) studied data from Tennessee elementary students. The purpose of their study was to "measure the relative magnitude of teacher effects while simultaneously considering the influences of intraclassroom heterogeneity, student achievement level, and class size on academic growth" (p. 58). The researchers examined scores

Guide to Transforming Teaching Through Self-Inquiry, pp. 7–14

from 1994 and 1995 for grades 3, 4, and 5; the scores were from five content areas: math, reading, language, social studies, and science. The results indicated that "the most important factor affecting student learning is the teacher" (p. 63). Additionally, classroom teachers "appear to be effective with students of all achievement levels, regardless of the level of heterogeneity in their classrooms" (p. 63).

Using some of the techniques from the Tennessee study, the Dallas Independent School District conducted a study of their students and the effect of teachers on student test scores (Haycock, 1998). This study, too, concluded that teachers have a significant effect on student achievement. As an example, the average reading scores for a group of fourth graders assigned to three highly effective teachers rose from a fourth-grade score in the 59th percentile to the 76th percentile by the end of sixth grade.

Haycock (1998) also examined a study that focused on high-school students in the Boston public schools. Bain and Company was contracted to study the scores on behalf of the district. Examining tenth-grade classrooms, the company found dramatic results. In reading, students taught by teachers ranked in the lower third of the district showed practically no gain, whereas students taught by teachers in the top third showed gains. In mathematics, the students taught by the bottom-third teachers showed virtually no gain, while students taught by the top-third teachers showed gains higher than the national average.

An important and interesting study was conducted by Nye, Konstantopoulos, and Hedges (2004) in which they examined data from a 4-year experiment that randomly assigned teachers and students to classes in order to estimate teacher effects on student achievement. While the study, like the other studies, points to the significance of the teacher, the authors made a critical point:

> We would argue that, because of random assignment of teachers and students to classrooms in this experiment, our results provide stronger evidence about teacher effects. The results of this study support the idea that there are substantial differences among teachers in the ability to produce achievement gains in their students. (Nye et al., 2004, p. 253)

Marzano, Marzano, and Pickering (2003) took a somewhat different approach. While the previous studies examined data acquired from students over a short period of time, Marzano et al. conducted a study using meta-analyses to synthesize research done over 35 years. This approach enabled the researchers to separate the effect of a school on student achievement from the effect of an individual teacher. Their results were startling. They concluded that a student in the 50th percentile who attends a school classified as least effective and has a teacher also classified as least effective will drop to the 3rd percentile after 2 years. In a more optimistic scenario, they concluded that a student in the 50th percentile who enters a school classified as effective and has a teacher classified as most effective will leave at the 96th percentile.

The importance of the teacher crosses international boundaries. In a mixed-methods study over 3 years, Sammons, Day, Kington, Gu, Stobart, and Smees (2007) designed and examined 300 case studies of teachers in grades 2, 6, and 9 in the United Kingdom. The results indicated that teachers had more influence than the schools themselves in accounting for differences in pupil progress. Yet Sammons and colleagues found other results that also deserve notice. In particular, their research detected "no evidence of a simple linear association between age or years of experience and teachers' relative effectiveness" (p. 692). This result has implications for the educator wishing to improve (and, indeed, for current arguments about tenure). *Experience, alone, is not enough.* Additionally, the study found that "teachers who are not committed and resilient are somewhat less likely to be effective in promoting pupils' academic outcomes" (p. 698). *Commitment, alone, also is not enough.*

It is therefore of the utmost importance to analyze exactly what teachers do on a daily basis so that we can begin to understand how we can ensure that teachers have a positive and lasting effect on their students.

2.2 Teacher Actions in the Classroom

Let us take a look at the everyday actions of a teacher. Belmonte, in discussing the role of the teacher, offers this startling summary:

> Wait until you stand in front of students, hundreds of them all day long. Five classes daily (if you're a high school teacher), 185 days or so per year, 50 minutes per class period: that's 45,000 minutes of class time. That's 15,000 3-minute speeches in one school year! (Belmonte, 2003, p. 8)

Belmonte's statement reminds us that teachers are literally making thousands of decisions annually.

In discussing the complexity of teaching, Ball and Cohen (1999) raise a salient point concerning teaching, namely, the ever-changing nature of classroom interactions and adaptations: "teaching occurs in particulars—particular students interacting with particular teachers over particular ideas in particular circumstances" (p. 10). Thus, effective teaching involves the "customizing" or the construction of teacher responses, and this "requires improvisation, conjecturing, experimenting, and assessing" (p. 10). According to Hunt (1976), the act of teacher adaptation to students "is the heart of the teaching-learning process" (p. 268). Teachers are constantly adapting to student moods, learning styles, time of day, administrative interruptions, and more. Hunt states that "teacher adaptation is occurring constantly, for example, a conservative estimate would be 100 occurrences per hour" (p. 268). This points to the *Constructivist nature of effective teaching*; teachers are continuously analyzing situations and creating mental schemes and behaviors to address an ever-changing class environment.

Adapting strategies, creating new strategies, and assessing the effectiveness of these constructs assume, of course, an existing framework. This framework, comprising teacher theories, guides the everyday actions of the teacher. Ross, Cornett, and McCutcheon (1992) view teacher theories as important because "teachers could not begin to practice without some knowledge of the context of their practice and some ideas about what can and should be done in those circumstances" (p. 3). But these theories are not static. McCutcheon (1992) tells us that teachers develop their theories through teaching ("practicing") and that "teachers keep working to enhance their proficiency and perfect their work further by increasing their expertise and their understanding of how students learn" (p. 191). Emphasizing the importance of the practical knowledge of teachers, Black and Halliwell (2000) state that "everyday teaching involves more complex decision-making than the one-way action of applying theory to practice" (p. 104). They point to the fact that teacher decision-making is "more like juggling, taking account of multiple, competing demands, assessing possibilities" (p. 104). The effective teacher is continuously creating new schemes and mental filters or personal theories.

Adding to the challenge of having to make myriad decisions and knowledge modifications on a daily basis is the necessity of infusing values into all teacher decisions. Gudmundsdottir (1990) notes: "The centrality of values in the pedagogical content of knowledge of experienced teachers should indicate to teacher educators that they need to address this important aspect of the knowledge of teaching" (p. 50). Under the umbrella of "values" Gudmundsdottir includes moral values, spiritual values, and worldly values, though he specifically discusses the first two. Moreover, he comments that experienced teachers should help new teachers make sure they include values in their decision-making.

Modifying theories, juggling priorities, adapting theories to particular situations and to particular students needs at a particular time, and infusing values into these decisions—all are activities requiring effective teachers to actively reflect upon their teaching.

2.3 A Closer Look at Reflection

The previous discussions set the stage for the importance of reflection. Only through the conscious act of reflecting can a teacher create new mental schemes to deal with the everchanging and contextual environment of the classroom. The reflecting process can be seen through different lenses as taking on different roles. Let's look at these roles.

One way in which reflection can be used is as an instrument for *creating personal theories*. Larrivee and Cooper (2006) states that among the many reasons educators may turn to reflection, the most important is "to deal with the inevitable uncertainties and tradeoffs involved in everyday decisions that affect the lives of students" (p. 1). Cole and Knowles (2000) also perceive reflection as the tool for creating personal teacher theories. They discuss two types of theory. The first type is global or macro in nature; it is often generated by researchers and is usually studied in teacher education programs. The second type of theory is micro or particular in nature; it usually emerges from the inquiry into one's beliefs and values. In discussing "reflexive practice" Cole and Knowles state that "the integration of elements or principles of both kinds of theories is the essence of reflexive or inquiring practice" (pp. 10-11).

Reflection can also be used as an *agent of change*. Argyris and Schön (1974) state that teachers, when asked about how they would act under certain conditions, usually give their espoused theory. On the other hand, a "theory-in-use" is the theory that *actually* governs a teacher's actions— and the reality is that these two theories may be incompatible. It is the teacher action of modifying espoused theories that results in the actual theory used. Argyris and Schön state that "few changes still can be made in schools and in practice unless faculties, students, and practitioners also become more aware of their espoused interpersonal theories and their interpersonal theories-in-use" (p. 180). This awareness is the product of teacher reflection.

Belmonte (2003) emphasizes passion in one's teaching practice but cautions that "passion must be connected to a plan" (p. 4). This plan consists of asking three important questions: What are you doing? Why you are doing it? And what must you do to improve it? Asking and answering these questions necessitates the use of reflection. Thus, reflection can be used as a *guide to direct passion* in the correct direction.

Engaging in practice that is structured by reflection also may enable the practitioner to avoid burnout and *create more autonomy*. Larrivee (2000) tells us that "routine action is guided by circumstance" (p. 2), whereas "reflective practice entails voluntarily and willingly taking responsibility for considering personal actions" (p. 2).

The importance of reflection is now ingrained in the culture of education. States across America have included reflection in professional teaching standards. For example, the Interstate Teacher Assessment and Support Consortium, a national organization, has created a document containing model core teaching standards. This document contains ten standards describing what effective teaching should be across all content areas and all grade levels. This document is grouped into four categories: (1) the learner and learning, (2) content, (3) instructional practice; and (4) professional responsibility. Teacher reflection is included in the category of professional responsibility. Also, many reflective actions are included throughout the standards.

2.4 Frameworks for Reflection

This section provides an analysis of different frameworks of reflection processes. While these frameworks can stand alone as separate entities, they can relate to each other.

Schön's (1983) framework examine the processes of reflection; he discusses *reflection in action,* which is observing, thinking, and acting as the experience is actually happening, and *reflection on action,* which is reflecting on a phenomenon after it has occurred, perhaps including one's feelings about the situation. Killion and Todnem (1991) add the concept of *reflection for action.* In reflection for action, the purpose is not to revisit a situation but to analyze it in order to guide future teacher actions and personal theories. A potential result of reflection for action is the transforming of one's teaching.

Suppose that a class is running smoothly, but then a normally well-behaved student yells out, "This is really boring; let's do something fun." This surprise or disequilibrium leads to reflection in action. Now the teacher must ask and answer questions such as "What do I do now?", "Why did he do that?", "How can I get the class back under control after this?", "Did I miss something here, or am I really being boring, and how do I make it more interesting?", or "Doesn't this student know that I do not allow such a thing?" These questions and subsequent answers are spontaneous and lead to a teacher reaction or new behavior that is done on the spot. This is reflection in action. Later, while driving home, the teacher starts thinking about the situation and asks himself about whether he noticed whether the student came in the room looking agitated, or whether he has allowed some students to shout out earlier, or whether he has not really focused in on reading the moods and body language of students. Further, he now considers having class discussions on the first day of class in order to ensure that students are fully aware of his expectations.

This is an example of reflection on action, reflecting on a past action in order to learn from this experience.

According to York-Barr, Sommers, Ghere, and Montie (2001), Van Manen (1977) proposed three levels to describe the aims of teacher reflection. The first level, *technical reflection,* looks at the skills, strategies, and methods used to reach goals. The second level, *practical reflection,* looks at the goals themselves. The third level, *critical reflection,* examines the moral, ethical, and social equity components of one's practice.

Now, let's look at the teacher from the previous discussion. When the teacher reflected about whether he was really boring and what he should do about that and how to get the class back under control, he was practicing technical reflection. When the teacher extends his reflecting to other areas and considers that he may have allowed some students to shout out earlier on in order not to appear "too strict," he realizes that what was supposed to be a positive gesture actually turned out to be a detriment. This is an example of practical reflection. Now suppose that the teacher considers focusing more on reading the moods of students and starts to consciously make this a priority; he also creates a plan to look for articles on the subject because he now believes that working with students on their feelings involves more important than content. This is an example of critical reflection.

2.5 Evolving From Reflection Into Inquiry

All effective teachers reflect. They reflect before, during, and after they are teaching. Teacher reflection is a daily activity, but it is different from teacher *inquiry.* While reflection is a part of teacher inquiry, they are different. As Dana and Yendol-Hoppey (2009) explain, inquiry involves intentionality; while reflection may be intentional at times, it is often done in an unplanned, informal way. It may done on the way to the teacher's lounge, it may be done while a teacher is eating lunch, it may be done while driving home, or it may be done while talking on the phone with a friend. Inquiry, on the other hand, involves the concept of *intentionality;* inquiry is the intentional act of reflecting on one's teaching practice.

A second difference that Dana and Yendol-Hoppey note is that inquiry is more visible. It is intentionally made more visible in forms such as journals, action research, professional portfolios, and professional development activities. When teachers intentionally reflect on their teaching and make this thinking visible in some form, then teachers are engaging in inquiry. It is this type of intentional and visible reflection or inquiry upon which this book focuses.

2.6 Summary

Figure 2.1 is a graphical version of what we have examined so far. We started with the most important reason for teaching: student learning. Research has indicated that the most crucial factor for learning is the teacher, and an examination of a teacher's daily routine indicated that effective teachers make hundreds of decisions concerning the multiple demands placed on them. Making decisions in such a complex and fast-paced classroom requires teachers to reflect on their practice and their theory-making. Teacher reflection, which involves technical, strategic, and ethical considerations, is often done in an informal and unplanned manner. When teacher reflection is done intentionally and is made visible in such tools such as journals, action research, and portfolios, it becomes inquiry. Teacher self-inquiry is the mechanism that can change the nature of or transform one's teaching practice and will, in turn, increase and deepen student learning.

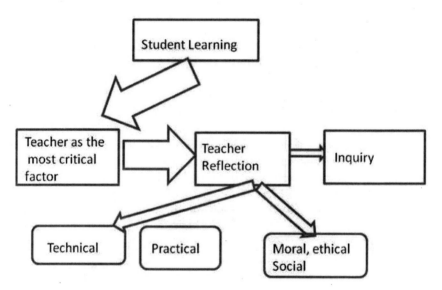

Figure 2.1.   The path to effective inquiry.

CHAPTER 3

FOUNDATIONS

In this chapter we examine different philosophies and theories and apply them to build a foundation for our system of teacher self-inquiry. We begin by summarizing what teachers do.

- What teachers do is structured not by abstract theories but by their everyday actions in the classroom.
- Teachers structure their practice on their personal theories.
- These personal theories are based on adjusting to the ever-changing situations in the classroom.
- Creating new mental schemes and behaviors in response to a flexible environment often results in conflicting theories or behaviors.
- Teachers infuse their values in the process of creating new personal theories and behaviors.

We need a theoretical framework that aligns with these ideas; in other words, we need a framework or philosophy that enables us to create a formal structure for the daily self-inquiry process of the teacher. That framework is *phenomenology.*

3.1 Teacher Self-Inquiry and Phenomenology

Phenomenology may be viewed in two ways (Stanford Encyclopedia of Philosophy, 2008): either as a disciplinary field or as a movement in the

---

Guide to Transforming Teaching Through Self-Inquiry, pp. 15–26
Copyright © 2013 by Information Age Publishing

history of philosophy. As a disciplinary field, it involves the study of the structures of experiences. Phenomenology "addresses the meaning things have in our experience, notably, the significance of objects, events, tools, the flow of time, the self, and others, as these things arise" (Stanford Encyclopedia of Philosophy, 2008, p. 2). Kleinman (2004), using the ideas of Giorgi (1997), views phenomenology as a method for examining a phenomenon "precisely as it is given or experienced in terms of the meaning that the phenomenon has for those experiencing it" (p. 8). Merleau-Ponty (2002) sees phenomenology as "the study of essences" (p. vii). We see that these definitions align nicely with teachers creating and reflecting on their own theories in order to respond to the fluid classroom environment. But the question arises, how can phenomenology help us create a system structuring teacher reflection and theorizing?

The answer lies in three important ideas presented in the cited definitions. The first is that our reflections and questions must focus on teacher experiences as they are happening. The second is that these experiences must be interpreted in terms of their meaning for the teacher. The third important concept, and the one we expand on below, is that of the essence of an experience.

Essence can be thought of as "the invariable aspects" (Sadala & Adorno, 2002, p. 286). It can also be thought of as the most important meaning of an experience in a particular context. Let us examine essence further by looking at the following journal entries:

> I was wondering how students would respond after missing class because of the snow. We are behind, but I really like doing those cooperative learning activities. They do take time.

In this instance the issue *seems to* be that of time. Now, let's look at the next entry, which is the result of focusing on the essence of the experience.

> I was wondering how students would respond after missing class because of the snow. We are behind, but I really like doing those cooperative learning activities. The reason I like them is that education students get to experience the activities that we preach about; they experience for themselves those "student-centered" activities we preach about. For me, the bottom line is modeling "best practices" and having preclinical students experience these activities—it is of paramount importance that they experience what we expect them to do as teachers. We (university professors) would not be doing our jobs otherwise.

Unlike the first example, the second example goes beneath the surface and looks at the underlying reason or assumptions for using cooperative learning activities. The most important meaning of this experience is the modeling of best practices, not that of time. The process of finding the essence of a phenomenon or event helps the educator find meaning in the experience.

3.2 Critical Reflection

While many people believe that critical reflection automatically results in a deeper reflection, Brookfield (1995) tells us that the "depth of a reflective effort does not, in and of itself, make it critical" (p. 8). He identifies two distinct purposes that make a reflection critical. The first is the consideration of how power issues frame and possibly distort educational practices and procedures. The second is the examination of our assumptions concerning practices and assumptions that are intended to make our teaching more effective but, in reality, do the opposite.

For example, as a secondary mathematics teacher I firmly believed in the effectiveness of cooperative learning activities. My belief was based on a presupposition of using cooperative learning, namely, that students are cognitively and emotionally ready to understand and integrate the ideas of others into their own thinking. But many interactions and discussions with students showed otherwise; many students indicated that listening to others confused them or that they personally were not ready to accept the ideas of others or that they were afraid that their partner would not perceive them as intelligent. What was initially thought of as being beneficial may, in reality, have had negative consequences. Using self-inquiry to examine the implementation of cooperative learning led me to question my assumption that cooperative learning is automatically effective. This questioning begins the process of changing the nature of one's teaching.

3.3 Transformative Learning

The word *transformation* can be defined as the process of changing the nature of something. We have seen how critical reflection starts the process of transforming one's teaching. In discussing transformation of living systems, including school systems, Marshall (2006) states that internal meaning change, not change from an external source, is "the source and catalyst for living system transformation" (p. 35). So, the nature of who we are as teachers begins with our own meaning-making. Osterman and Kottkamp (1993) complement this idea. In discussing the change process they state that change will take place when the individual understands the relationship between their personal theories and an unacceptable performance or result. Both of these examples point to the individual internalizing the need for change, and this is the start of transformation.

Now let's take this one step further. Mezirow (1991) states that "reflective learning becomes transformative whenever assumptions or premises are found to be distorting, inauthentic, or otherwise invalid" (p. 6). By examining underlying assumptions, one starts the process of changing one's teaching; new meaning perspectives result, and one's teaching is transformed.

Consider the following entry that I made in my journal.

> Nov. 2nd—The last couple of weeks, things have seemed to become smoother.... Also, I felt that it was not necessary to act as intensely enthusiastically as I had in the past. I am waiting for them to do this. While I have tried consciously to work on letting the students take responsibility for creating an enthusiastic environment—purposely staying more "even-keeled" and looking for their reaction. I felt that I may become naturally less enthusiastic, and changing for the worst. Am I losing my teaching persona?

This entry describes a possible disequilibrium, but there is no indication that a change may be imminent. However, the next day's entry presents the beginning of the process of creating a new meaning scheme.

> Nov. 3rd—thought about allowing students "pick up the pace" when it comes to enthusiasm. It may be a case of seeing my role change. While, at first, it was for me to model being enthusiastic, now it may be the time to gradually pull away from the role of role model, it might be best if I discuss this with them ... maybe about how they must be more enthusiastic in class, and let me feed off their energy. They will need to know how to show enthusiasm every minute, every day. It may be about having a plan where I slowly shift from role model to observer, participant, and maybe even mentor.

This leads to another concept that Mezirow discusses: the concept of taking action. He defines reflective action as "making decisions or taking other action predicated upon the insights resulting from reflection" (p. 108). Let's take a closer look at the process of having knowledge flow into action.

3.4 Knowledge and Action

Pfeffer and Sutton (2000) discuss the paradox that, while many companies talk about the knowledge needed to succeed in their businesses, they frequently fail to take the necessary steps to turn that knowledge into action. In discussing competitive advantage, they write that people "can read a book or attend a seminar. The trick is in turning the knowledge acquired into organizational action" (p. 25). A complementary principle is that one can "learn by doing as well as by reading and thinking" (p. 25). This principle is critical because it tells us that one can learn through experience. Pfeffer and Sutton expand on this by stating that the acquisition of knowledge "through practice, performance, and even failure is indispensable for organizations of all sizes and types" (p. 27). The "business" of teaching can benefit from the ideas of Pfeffer and Sutton. Teachers can reflect on their own theories, examine the efficacy of those theories in the classroom, and use self-inquiry to modify and apply their new theories. It is through such action that present knowledge is transformed into new knowledge. And the process is an iterative one.

3.5 Asking Questions

Questioning plays an essential role in the transformation process. The act of asking questions can change or transform your teaching life. Leeds (2000) states that "it is the act of questioning that causes us to go deep inside and examine our emotional selves" (p. 1). Leeds's ideas also align with our belief that knowledge by itself is ineffectual; rather, it is the process of turning knowledge into action that is most important. Leeds states that questioning can empower us to "take actions that turn our lives around" (p. 1).

Goldberg (1998) extends the importance of questioning to include its role in the creativity process: "Every creative act thus begins implicitly or explicitly with a genuine question" (p. 9). Considerable creativity is involved in transforming one's practice, and questioning thus is a critical tool.

3.6 Characteristics of Reflective Thinking

Since teacher self-inquiry requires teacher reflection, let us examine the characteristics of the reflective teacher. We will call first on the ideas of Dewey. Farrell (2004) discusses Dewey's three characteristics of reflection:

- Open-mindedness
- Responsibility
- Wholeheartedness

The ability to see events and concepts from a different perspective and to consider and integrate alternative viewpoints forms the foundation for open-mindedness. As a reflective educator, responsibility requires focusing your behavior on the improvement of student learning. Wholeheartedness means viewing your lived experience as an opportunity to learn about your students and how to help them learn.

Costa and Garmston (1994) offer five states of mind for the reflective educator. We will use three of them:

- Efficacy
- Consciousness
- Craftsmanship

Efficacy is the firm knowing that you, as the teacher, can make a difference. Consciousness is the process of cognitively monitoring the environment around you. Craftsmanship is the constant focus on and the desire for improvement in your teaching.

These characteristics not only help define the persona of the reflective educator; they also help structure the reflection process. These characteristics will help create the prompts we'll examine that will, in turn, help your reflect on your teaching.

3.7 Constructivism

Until now we have discussed how teachers improve their teaching and improve student learning by reflecting on their teaching, with the following four aims:

- understanding the essence and meanings of their teaching experiences;
- examining the underlying assumptions and meaning schemes of one's teaching;
- creating new mental and meaning schemes in order to understand new situations; and
- putting into action the knowledge created through the newly created schemes, and using the experience to further modify the knowledge.

These four aims each include the embedded concept that you, as a teacher, must understand and interpret your teaching experience and use this experience to create new meaning schemes and new personal theories.

But how does a teacher do this? What is the nature of the new knowledge created? What are the mechanics of analyzing the results of implementing a new teaching theory? And what if one's personal theories do not answer a novel teaching situation? All these questions require the assumption that knowledge, such as the knowledge we are discussing in the teacher self-inquiry process, is *created*, as opposed to being passed on. Here, the Constructivist philosophy will guide us in our analysis.

Constructivism is not pedagogy; rather, it is a philosophy about how one learns (Pelech & Pieper, 2010). While many definitions and versions of the Constructivist philosophy exist, they share the following beliefs:

- People create their own knowledge, rather than receiving or transmitting knowledge.
- Knowledge is created by connecting the new experience to previous knowledge.
- Knowledge is an autonomous and subjective construction.
- Learning involves a restructuring of one's thinking schemes.
- Knowledge is created through personal experiences and social interaction.
- Cognitive growth is activated with practical, contextual problems requiring a new way to think.

3.7.1 Principles of Learning

Clearly, the Constructivist philosophy contains many ideas that align with our views of reflection. Therefore, let's look at some principles of Constructivism (Pelech & Pieper, 2010):

Learning Principle 1: Students learn by participating in activities that enable them to create their own version of knowledge. This includes creating rules, definitions, and experiments.
Learning Principle 2: Students learn when they teach others, explain to others, or demonstrate a concept to others.
Learning Principle 3: Students learn when they create products from the real world that involve narratives, explanations, justifications, and dialogue.
Learning Principle 4: Knowledge comes in multiple forms, and its development is not uniform; hence, students must be given the opportunity to develop each intelligence or domain.
Learning Principle 5: Students learn when class activities stimulate multiple senses.
Learning Principle 6: Students learn by creating knowledge at different levels of complexity and thinking.
Learning Principle 7: Students learn by connecting new experiences with existing knowledge or connecting previously discrete experiences to each other.

Learning Principle 8: Students learn when they are continuously presented with problems, questions, or situations that force them to think differently.

Learning Principle 9: Students learn by making connections through the "Standard Six": compare and contrast, hypothesize and predict, express understanding in multiple modes, find patterns, summarize, and find personal relevance.

Learning Principle 10: Students regulate their learning by (1) knowing their own ability and learning style preference, (2) analyzing tasks and appropriate strategies, (3) choosing and analyzing appropriate goals, (4) analyzing and appraising their individual level of performance, and (5) managing their time effectively.

Learning Principle 11: Students learn by working with other people who are the source of contradiction, different perspectives, and confirmation.

Learning Principle 12: Modern society provides the source of authentic products for students to produce.

These principles can be used to create strategies for transforming your teaching. We will now start the process of doing this.

3.7.2 Four Important Metaphors

In this section we analyze our Constructivist principles and create metaphors that will help us develop prompts for reflecting and using self-inquiry.

We begin with Principles 1, 2, 10, and 11. The common theme is that of *autonomy*. All four of these principles can be blended together to create the concept of autonomy. For the educator, autonomy means that you, as the teacher, take responsibility for, control, and evaluate all that goes on in the classroom and recognize that you are the most important element of student success. Autonomy means "being captain of your ship." This metaphor includes teacher characteristics and teacher personal theories; see Figure 3.1.

As we discussed earlier, a foundation of our system is that of lived experience. This implies that reflections will dwell on authentic experiences and instruments, the experiences and instruments used in the everyday teaching. Blending Principles 3, 4, and 12 and creating a theme of real-life experiences, we arrive at the "TV reality show" metaphor as illustrated in Figure 3.2. Just as a TV reality show depicts experiences as they are lived, including people's reactions to these experiences, so too do reflections in our system depict teachers' lived experiences and the meaning these experiences have.

Our model of reflection and self-inquiry includes the creation and modification of the teacher's personal theories and the creation of new

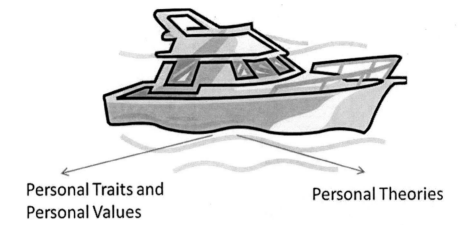

Personal Traits and
Personal Values

Personal Theories

Figure 3.1.   Being captain of your ship.

mental spaces or knowledge bases. What are the mechanics of this process? And what is the nature of knowledge, especially teacher knowledge? Principles 5, 6, 7, and 9 address these questions. We see that Principle 5 deals with using multiple senses to learn, Principle 6 deals with different forms of knowledge, and Principles 7 and 9 deal with the framework and mechanics of creating new knowledge. To these principles we add the concept that real knowledge is the turning of ideas into action; this is represented through an action plan. Applying each of these principles to a

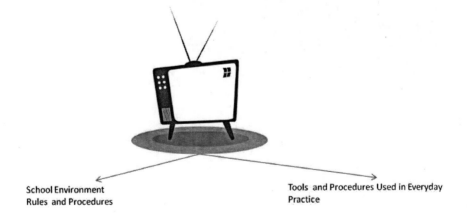

School Environment
Rules and Procedures

Tools and Procedures Used in Everyday
Practice

Figure 3.2.   TV reality show and responding to experiences.

Create and
evaluate a plan

Personal Relevance

Summarize

Find and
Use Patterns

Multiple Modes

Hypothesize
and Predict

Compare
and
contrast

Figure 3.3.   Turn the kaleidoscope.

new experience will result in a new perspective or a lived experience and possibly new mental and emotional schemes. Emphasizing the concept of "new perspective" is represented by the "turn the kaleidoscope" metaphor (See Figure 3.3).

We can see that these cognitive activities are fundamental to transforming one's daily teaching. As educators you can use these activities to analyze everyday classroom experiences and create mental spaces that will eventually transform your teaching practice.

This transformation process begins with some form of *disequilibrium*. It can be a usually effective teaching practice that is not working or a gut feeling that something just isn't right. It can be a teaching practice that is research-based but with your students seems to be hurting student learning. It can come from power or gender issues (critical reflection) such as the fact that only females are responding positively to a certain activity. Disequilibrium, which evolves from Principle 8, can be seen as getting one's attention or, in the popular vernacular, "rattling your cage" (see Figure 3.4).

Each of these metaphors, or prompts, empowers educators to focus on an aspect of their everyday practice in order to determine whether a change is necessary or what area or issue needs to be addressed. The process of disequilibrium—far from being negative—starts the process of transformation.

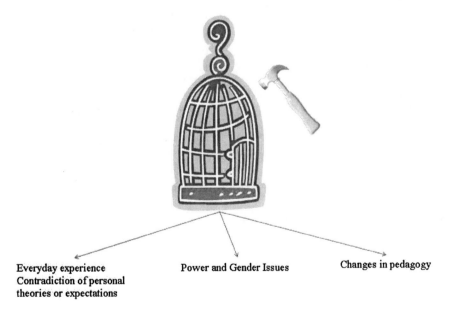

Everyday experience
Contradiction of personal
theories or expectations

Power and Gender Issues

Changes in pedagogy

Figure 3.4.   Rattling your cage.

3.8 Summary

To understand one's teaching and how to transform it so one becomes a more effective teacher, we start with concepts from phenomenology and examine the everyday life of the teacher. This process includes examining the assumptions, beliefs, and values underlying one's teaching. The objective is to transform one's teaching by constructing new theories, beliefs, and teaching practices. These new constructs are then put into action, thus restarting the cycle. Figure 3.5 illustrates this process.

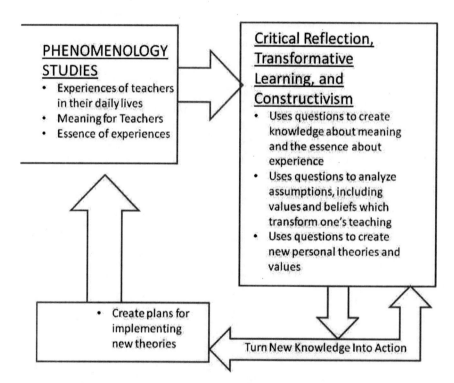

Figure 3.5.   Constructing knowledge and putting it into action.

CHAPTER 4

THE SYSTEM

In this chapter we build on the foundations and concepts discussed in
Chapter 3. This chapter is essential to our study of teacher self-inquiry
because self-inquiry means that the teacher makes reflections intentional
and visible. In this chapter we discuss some ways for accomplishing this.

4.1 Platforms for Self-Inquiry

Platforms are the tools that will make one's reflection visible. Moreover,
they have the capability of actually structuring the reflection/inquiry process. While many platforms for inquiry exist, we will examine the following:

- Journals and journal variations
- Interactive journals
- Portfolios
- Action research
- Professional development

4.2 Prompts for Self-Inquiry

No matter what platform is chosen, there must be some guidelines, or
prompts, that can be used to structure one's inquiry. We present our

Guide to Transforming Teaching Through Self-Inquiry, pp. 27–31
Copyright © 2013 by Information Age Publishing
All rights of reproduction in any form reserved.

prompts in the form of questions, which we derive from our foundations of phenomenology, critical reflection, transformative learning, the knowledge/action relationship, and the characteristics of a reflective teacher. Professional educators who review and use these prompts will be successful at transforming their teaching practice. We will start with the four Constructivist metaphors presented in Chapter 3.

4.2.1 Autonomy—Be Captain of Your Ship

The "captain of your ship" metaphor focuses on autonomy. We've associated two types of prompts with this metaphor, as shown in Figure 4.1. The prompts labeled "Personal Traits" emerge from blending autonomy with the characteristics of a reflective teacher, while the prompts labeled "Personal Theories" are the result of blending autonomy with phenomenology, transformative learning, and critical assumptions and values.

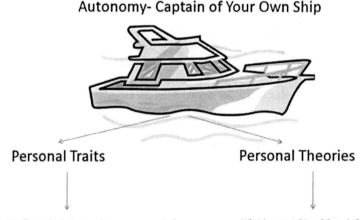

Autonomy- Captain of Your Own Ship

Personal Traits

- Am I willing to look at more than one perspective?
- Is "student learning" my focus?
- Do I see every classroom event as an opportunity to help students?
- Do I believe that my reflections will help students learn?
- Am I satisfied with my teaching? If ss was discussed the "Cions of Pdgengng the efficacy of those tehories in the cl lobably better. I just may have missed it. tho, why?
- Am I a problem solver or a standard enforcer?
- Am I willing to change your mental schemes for interpreting classroom events?
- Am I willing to self-monitor (reflect?)

Personal Theories

- What is my teaching philosophy?
- What are my personal theories?
- What mental schemes do you use for interpreting class events?
- Where did my theories come from?
- Where did my mental schemes come from?
- What do I do without thinking?
- What are my core values as a teacher?
- What ideological assumptions have I made?

Figure 4.1.   Blending autonomy with personal concepts—being captain of your ship.

4.2.2 Lived Experiences—TV Reality Show

Since the actual lived experiences of teachers are the focus of transformative inquiry, these prompts create the stage on which the transformation will take place. Pairing this theme with phenomenology, critical assumptions, and transformative learning results in the prompts shown in Figure 4.2.

4.2.3 Turn the Kaleidoscope—Creating New Mental Schemes and Theories

Transformative inquiry includes examining the core values and critical assumptions that frame one's practice. It also implies creating mental and emotional filters in order to eliminate the actions that have proved ineffective, and then initiating new actions to transform one's teaching. The prompts for this metaphor are shown in Figures 4.3a and 4.3b.

The transformation process often begins with disequilibrium—a surprise, a disappointing result, an unexpected event, an event different from the norm. Or, the process can begin when present schemes are unable to address a situation. The prompts are shown in Figure 4.4.

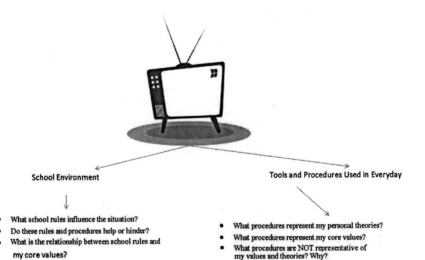

School Environment

- What school rules influence the situation?
- Do these rules and procedures help or hinder?
- What is the relationship between school rules and my core values?

- What is the school environment for change?
- What latitude do I have for innovation?

Tools and Procedures Used in Everyday

- What procedures represent my personal theories?
- What procedures represent my core values?
- What procedures are NOT representative of my values and theories? Why?
- What artifacts represent my values and personal theories?
- Which artifacts are the most important to me?
- What theories or procedures am I not?

Figure 4.2.   Lived experience—TV reality show.

4.3 Summary

Transforming one's teaching begins with self-inquiry. This chapter has provided a wide range of prompts that can be used or modified in conjunction with self-inquiry. These prompts are designed to enable you to analyze and transform your own teaching in order to help students learn and transform their lives. The prompts can be used on any platform for inquiry, as we discuss in the next chapter.

Compare and Contrast	Find and Use Patterns	Multiple Modes	Hypothesize and Predict

- How does this compare with past problems?
- What is bothering me?
- How is this class different from others?
- How have I changed with this class? Why?
- How does this conflict with my personal theories?
- How does this conflict with my core values?
- How do class artifacts of what we actually do? compare or conflict with my personal theories?
- What patterns of behavior are occurring?
- What patterns are seen through class artifacts?
- What patterns conflict with my personal theories?
- What patterns align with my personal theories or core values?
- Why am I feeling differently?
- How do my personal theories used in this class compare with theory of published research?

- What types of modes do I use in my teaching?
- What platform or mode will I use to reflect?
- What produced this result or relationship?
- What do I need to change in order to succeed?
- What meaning does this have for me?
- For transformation?
- What do I know? What do I need to know?
- What resources do I need to use?
- What theory can I use?
- What part of my personal theory do I change?
- What would happen if...?
- What do I think will happen if I...
- Do these proposed new personal theories align with or contradict my original theories?
- Will these proposed changes transform my teaching?

Figure 4.3a.   Turn the kaleidoscope—examining core values and critical assumptions.

Summarize	Personal Relevance	Create and Evaluate a Plan

- What have I learned that can help my students?
- What has surprised me? Why?
- What is missing from my reflection?
- Where am I now with regard to my question?
- What do I still need to do?
- What tools do I need to still use?
- Do I need to change directions?
- Where am I in terms of the transformation process?
- What artifacts represent transformation? Why?
- What meaning does this have for me?
- What doesn't have meaning for me? Why?
- Have my meaning schemes helped me with this situation?
- Do I need to redefine what is relevant for me?

- What is the present situation?
- What are my present resources?
- What is my goal?
- Do my goals help me transform my practice?
- What is my plan to reach the goal?
- What are alternative plans to reach the goal?
- What are the helping forces?
- What are the hindering forces?
- What action steps do I choose?
- What outside sources can help me?

Figure 4.3b.   Turn the kaleidoscope—forming a plan of action.

- What surprised me?
- What did I not anticipate?
- Is there something about my personal theories that I am not comfortable with?
- Could my assumptions about power and equity not be applicable?
- What if I looked at things from a different perspective?

- Is there another explanation for my frustration?
- Are my core values being questioned?
- Are my personal theories being challenged?
- What aspects of my personal theories could be changed to help this situation?
- What about my plan should be adjusted?
- What goals are irrelevant to this situation?
- What if...?

Figure 4.4.   Rattling your cage—responding to disequilibrium.

CHAPTER 5

TEACHER JOURNALS

Taking many formats, teacher journals provide educators with a platform to monitor, critique, and design actions to transform their teaching. In particular, journals provide transformational factors such as time to reflect on one's practice, review one's growth and research, prepare to perform more effectively in the future, and examine the gap between knowledge and behavior.

5.1 Purposes of Teacher Journals

Teachers keep journals for two main reasons: strategic and pedagogical. From a strategic point of view, using a journal provides many advantages. Connelly and Clandinin (1990) see journals as locating information within the context of teaching: "Journals made by participants in the practical setting are [a] source of data in narrative inquiry" (p. 5). Journals help provide teachers with a deeper understanding of what they do every day in the school setting, especially in the classroom. Farrell (2004) views journals as helping us to "freeze our work so we that we can reflect deliberately on it" (p. 74). According to York-Barr, Sommers, Ghere, and Montie (2001), journaling "offers a private place for honest accounting and review" (p. 52). It can also "bring many events together in one place, helping us to see their interrelations" (Cell, 1984, p. 222). The journal can bridge the gap between one's knowledge and action (Collier, 1999)

Guide to Transforming Teaching Through Self-Inquiry, pp. 33–52
Copyright © 2013 by Information Age Publishing
33

and can help one better monitor classroom events (Maloney & Campbell-Evans, 2002). Thus, the journal can help one perform more effectively by preparing one "to benefit more from … future experience" (Cell, 1984, p. 226).

From the pedagogical point of view, writing in a journal can serve many practical purposes. Journals can be running accounts of important events and can be used to raise questions about experiences (Osterman & Kottkamp, 1993). Dobbins (1996), in her study on student teachers, found benefits of teacher journaling such as confronting broader educational issues, understanding their feelings, and solving teaching problems. In describing case studies of preservice teachers, Spalding and Wilson (2002) write that some of the benefits of journals include providing a safe outlet for frustrations and concerns and serving as a tool for internal dialogue. Equally important, the journal can provide evidence for the *absence* of reflective thinking (Wong, Kember, Chung, & Yan, 1995). It can help the educator recognize that certain situations have been ignored (such as my experience in not acknowledging that group activities might not be benefiting the students) and can enable teachers to become more aware of their own prejudices and biases (Larrivee, 2000).

5.2 Platforms and Modes for Journals: An Overview

Is there a special form that a teacher journal must take? Farrell (2004) tells us that the journal can be a handwritten note, a private journal, or an interactive exchange with a critical friend. The 21st century has provided new platforms and tools for communicating. It is important that teachers utilize the different acceptable modes and tools that students will be using in their lifetime. These modes include both audio and visual. Johnson (2002) encourages teachers to "take up opportunities to extend classroom knowledge to reflective practice" (p. 388). While the visual mode is increasingly becoming a platform for instruction, it can also be used for teacher reflection. And, with the introduction of technology such as digital recorders and webcams, a journal can be audio-recorded. Such journals can enable educators to literally see or hear themselves in action.

Let us now take a closer look at these different platforms and their advantages and disadvantages as teacher journals.

5.2.1 Audio Recordings and Journal Entries

A tape recorder, compared with the written word, provides the advantage of documenting a great amount of information. Seidman (2006) discusses the advantages of tape-recording interviews; his ideas can be applied to digital recorders and teacher reflections. He reminds us that "the participants' thoughts become embodied in their words" (p. 114). Seidman also points to the advantage that the teacher can go back and listen to the tape in order to clarify any points. Audio recordings also provide the advantage of enabling the teacher to listen to voice pitch and tone.

Nevertheless, using audio recording of reflections does have some disadvantages. The tape must be transcribed, a process that can be both long and tedious. While there are solutions to this problem, they may not be desirable, and may even be counterproductive. One solution is to pick out the parts that seem to be the most important. Doing so, however, may lead to a premature judgment of what the reflection is really portraying, as the real context of the message may be lost. Another solution is that of using a voice recognition (VR) program. Batt and Wilson (2008) discuss the advantages and disadvantages of VR programs in a study of responses to student writing. The results indicated that the VR program provided value for producing end comments but proved ineffective for the editing and revising that were part of the study.

5.2.2 Video Journal Entries

Biology tells us that video can offer many advantages over audio. Why? Burmark (2002), in discussing the concept of visual literacy, cites the data presented by Lindstrom (1999); he tells us that our two optic nerves consist of 1,000,000 nerve fibers, whereas each auditory nerve contains 30,000 fibers. Additionally, nerve cells dedicated to visual processing make up about 30% of the cortex of the brain, whereas cells for touch account for only 8% and hearing for even less, only 3%.

Clarke (2009) discusses the advantages of video journaling. Videos can convey emotions and complexity more effectively than can text, videos are more effective in an online environment, and videos can enable the teacher to develop technology communication skills that can then be put to action in the classroom.

Clarke also acknowledges, however, that using video reflections has some disadvantages. There is the possibility that the reflection can come from a prepared script (the teacher may want to "look good"), and there is the possibility that technical issues may overshadow the effectiveness of video reflections.

Given the potential disadvantages raised by Clarke, let us therefore look at some research on the effectiveness of the visual mode. We will focus on a particular type of visual mode, the graphical organizer.

Graphical organizers are tools used to organize information and knowledge through pictures, diagrams, or graphics. Alvermann (1981) showed that graphical organizers were significant when tenth-grade students were required to reorganize information after reading an expository passage. More recently, a study by Harpaz, Balik, and Ehrenfeld (2004) focused on concept mapping in nursing education. Concept maps are visual/graphical tools that use geometrical shapes such as boxes or circles to show relationships between concepts. Related concepts have a line connecting them to indicate their relationship. Concept maps are used in all types of content areas besides nursing education, and I have used them in my university education courses and in my middle school math courses at Saint Ethelreda School. At the end of each semester students and instructors were asked to evaluate the efficiency of the teaching/learning process using concept mapping. The researchers reported that students believed that concept mapping encouraged independent thinking, improved their ability in making connections between different areas, and increased their confidence in applying knowledge in clinical work. Moreover, the nursing teachers believed that concept mapping helped in integrating material and enabled students to become active learners.

While we have established some documented benefits of the visual mode, a natural question is how the visual mode can be used effectively in *teacher reflection*. Garner (1997), in describing a study of special education teachers who used different forms of representation to present their understandings of their own institution as a part of in-service training courses, concluded that teachers can "use graphics as triggers to their understanding of the work they do" (p. 281). Teachers were asked to create perceptions of their work places through drawings. These drawings also included concept maps. Teachers also included written reflections with their visual tools. Johnson (2001) studied the effects of having seventeen preservice secondary teachers create visual narratives (picture books). The results of the study indicated that "visual metaphor is a viable alternative to literal written description or personal journal writing when reflecting on professional matters" (p. 136). However, the preservice teachers in this study did not demonstrate a change in their overall perceptions.

A possible solution to this dilemma comes from another study done by Johnson (2004); this study examined the effects of using a visual-verbal means for conducting reflective inquiry. Johnson states: "In most cases where teacher drawings are accompanied by written or spoken text, the research has concluded that visual-verbal language offers greater possibilities for understanding teacher identity than is possible through a single source" (pp. 423-424).

In a study by Black and Halliwell (2000) fourteen Australian early childhood teachers who worked in privately owned centers took part in a collaborative inquiry project to examine everyday teaching actions. Feedback from participating teachers "claimed it was liberating to think and talk about teaching using drawing, metaphor, conversation, and reflective journal writing" (p. 112).

Both these last two studies suggest the power of *combining* different modes.

5.2.3 A Closer Look at Narrative

Narrative, written and spoken, has been an important tool for reflection. Let us therefore look at it in more detail. Watson and Wilcox (2000) argue that careful readings of the way in which people present their experiences to themselves enable them to develop a deeper understanding of their practice. To help the practitioner, Watson and Wilcox present two reflective methods. The first method "invites practitioners to read their *stories* of practice, examining how we have made sense of our professional experience through narrative" (p. 57). Our discussion of narrative inquiry provides us with the prompts for this.

The second method "encourages practitioners to read their *conventions* of practice, examining how we have ordered our professional experiences through particular strategies, approaches, and routines" (Watson & Wilcox, 2000, pp. 57-58). In this second approach, the practitioner collects artifacts representative of the day-to-day routines; these artifacts, such as lesson plans, handouts, syllabi, rules, student work, and letters, are documentation of how a practitioner goes about daily practice. The next step, according to Watson and Wilcox, is annotation, for which they recommend such prompts as the following:

- What are the origins of the routine?
- What are the purposes of the routines or conventions?
- What is the significance of the routine or convention?

Additionally, the prompts from Chapter 4 will serve to annotate the significance of the artifacts. The final stage, reassembling the artifacts, can be derived from the prompts or derivations of these prompts. Possible prompts or combination of prompts follow:

- What if I looked at it from the perspective of___?
- How are these artifacts related or not related to each other?

- What meanings do these artifacts have for me?
- Does this represent practice that is different from what I profess to believe in? If so, what new belief, perspective, or practice do I need to create?

5.3 Examples of Traditional Journal Entries

In this section we present examples of teacher journaling. We use our principles and frameworks to analyze these different examples. Some of the journal entries have been edited for clarity, but the editing has not altered the important points and characteristics of the reflection.

5.3.1 Description

The first example comes from a Measurement and Evaluation class at the college level. In this class I have students personally experience some of the different instruments for assessing students. In this case I had students create their own portfolio on what they had learned during the first 3 weeks of this class. Figure 5.1 contains the reflection.

> *After talking with one of my students today, a couple of other ideas came up which I want to talk about. This student stated that from her observation many of her classmates did not use a digital format for their portfolio. Also, in a related matter, I found out that many students were not sure what was meant by the term "artifact." They sure seem shy and not ready to try things such as a digital portfolio.*

Figure 5.1.   Description.

Analysis: In this example I describe a problem but leave the reflection at this level. This reflection does not question why students were afraid to try a digital portfolio or were hesitant to clarify what an artifact is. This entry does not discuss a plan to address these issues. As this journal entry is merely a summary of events, it is in no way a vehicle for transformation.

5.3.2 Content and Process

The second example, also from my Measurement and Evaluation class, examines a trend that had bothered me for a considerable time. I was concerned with students not reading the required articles, so for the past few years I have started each class with a quiz. However, the students in this class were not doing as well as I wanted on the quizzes. Here, as shown by Figure 5.2, is the journal entry for this class:

Students seemed more ready for the quiz. They (more students) came in early and quizzed each other. There was more of a serious tone. I did notice an improvement in most scores, though it was an easier quiz. Some students are still struggling with quizzes … Some are still confused on ____ model of intelligence and the book's definition of performance assessment. Might be time for some direct instruction. I want to start connecting our class activities to solving the Problematic. I am assuming they are doing this on their own, and this is the initiative I want, but if one values formative assessment [discussing possible student solution in class] this should be done continuously. So I am trying to balance initiative and formative assessment … This begs the question, how does my teaching philosophy balance this?

Figure 5.2.   Focus beyond description.

Analysis: This reflection goes beyond the description phase to focus on process and content. The process of giving quizzes to ensure that students have read the material is confirmed, but this is not transformative learning. It is assumed that quizzing students will motivate them to read and study and hence increase their quiz scores. The second part of the reflection brings up some disequilibrium because it demonstrates a "disconnect" between my desire to provide the students with initiative and my belief in formative assessment. The reflection presents the disequilibrium in the form of a question. Raising this question starts the process of transforming my practice because it encourages me to create new "mental space" or scheme in my teaching philosophy, a scheme that connects and blends formative assessment with student initiative.

5.3.3 Questioning Fairness and Creating a Tool to Transform Practice

Here is another example from my college class. In this class I was conducting action research on student time management, a concern I have in teaching my college classes. One student suggestion was to take a major assignment and break it into smaller increments or benchmarks. Further, I was to grade these smaller assignments formatively (no grade, just comments for improvement) and then hand them back to the students. Approximately twelve students volunteered and finished this "experiment." As straightforward as this initiative seemed, problems did arise. Let's look at Figure 5.3.

I'm thinking about the "experiment" I am doing with my class ... but a bigger problem has arisen. While I assess this formatively, sending suggestions, I am torn with the thought that I may be hurting students. I see trends that need to be addressed ... they are all making the same mistakes, and I feel obliged to discuss this with the entire class, but here's the catch—only some of the class volunteered to do this. So, they do the work and others benefit? I know the students volunteering, for the most part, worked entirely hard and did get my feedback. The others will now be the beneficiaries [if I discuss the trends I saw] of this work. Is this really fair? I know, community, community, but my gut is telling me something different. It just doesn't seem right. Now, if the entire class was to doing this that would be different. Where do I draw the line? Of course, on the other hand, some of the students who chose not to participate did so because their schedules did not allow them to participate. So, should they be punished? I just don't have the framework (mentally or emotionally) to think about this. I guess I could use the process from Problem Based Learning. Here is my emerging new mental construct or framework, "How can I develop a system of rough drafts or benchmarked/chunked assignments such that I am fair to everyone, no one rides the coattails of others?"

This question is my starting point. Now what do I do? What is my plan? I should possibly talk to former students, or even the students participating in this, talk to the rest of my department, talk to my colleagues at other schools. In fact, maybe this should be an item in my Yearly plan.

Figure 5.3.   Disequilibrium.

Analysis: In this reflection we observe both disequilibrium and incoherence that is caused by questioning the assumption of fairness of a practice intended to help students. This reflection represents the pathway to transforming my practice. I not only challenge an underlying assumption, I start the process of creating a new mental framework by formulating a plan to develop this framework.

5.3.4 Hegemony

The next example originated from my middle-school teaching at Saint Ethelreda School. In my teaching and mentoring there I have used cooperative learning activities, and I have also taught the students some mental math tricks. Figure 5.4 contains part of this reflection.

Their response in class surprised me. They said that "Pair/Share" was boring! Wow! Then, immediately they wanted to do mental math ... While I was excited I wondered how I could design mental math exercises to align with the standardized tests. I am about autonomy, so I've decided to do this: I will do a "scale model" problem like the ones from the sample questions, and have them add up the numbers in their head. I am about math in context and autonomy. I really feel they are more excited about the mental math. What I will do is this: First review how to do this mentally (go left to right) 32 +43—30+40= 70 and 2 + 3 = 5-75. Then they would determine the distances in a problem such as:

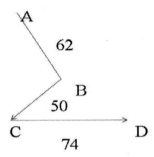

I then would have them add 60 + 50 + 70= 180, 2+ 0 + 4= 6, 186 miles. Scale problems are on the test, and the mental math helps with their autonomy.

Figure 5.4.   Hegemony.

Analysis: This journal entry is an example of reflection for action. It starts to address the process of transformation by redefining and modifying core values. It blends student autonomy (a core value) with the preparation for state tests; this newly formed mental scheme could be fully developed into a defining core value. Regarding Van Manen's framework, this reflection is at the practical level, though the comment about aligning with the state tests indicates there may be an ethical or moral issue concerning preparing students for the state exams.

5.3.5 Technical Knowledge and Core Values and Goals

Initially, some of the students in my class were shy about answering open-ended questions. They were used to "right or wrong" questions and often would not answer an open-ended question or would say "I don't know." I tried a Constructivist approach, therefore, of using small groups. Figure 5.5 is one of my later journal reflections.

Things flowed better. They chose partners quickly and divided up work quickly. I am more comfortable with integrating my Constructivist activities into the course. I am experiencing less of "I don't know" and more of an attitude of taking a risk. I realize that I really coach emotions ... Hmmm ... maybe in teacher preparation programs we should look more at training teachers to coach mindsets.

Figure 5.5.   Technical knowledge and core values.

Analysis: This journal entry starts off with a description and then moves to a technical analysis by noting that more Constructivist-type activities have been introduced. The entry touches on core values by mentioning the realization that a teacher actually coaches emotions. While the reflection does not develop this thought, it does raise the possibility of considering this later on. Additionally, the entry mentions that the coaching of one's emotions should possibly be a part of teacher preparation programs. This represents not only a change in or addition to goals but a potential change in core values.

5.4 Examples of Less Traditional Journals

This section departs from the traditional "paper and pencil" journal. The examples presented here include transcripts from audio journals, graphical organizers with reflections, artifacts and reflections, handwritten notes, and cartoons. All these cases, however, involve some type of written reflection.

5.4.1 Using a Voice Recognition Program

Let us begin with an actual transcript of a voice recognition program, as shown in Figure 5.6.

Great. The program seems to be working. I am in the classroom and talking about my assessment class. Today was a pretty good day. Many students came in early for the quizzes and did quite well with is, so I wonder what is really motivating them to do this. You know what I am really thinking about? They are working very well in their groups. I want to know how much longer before I change groups. Two more? They really are working nicely, and I do not want to lose momentum. Also, trying very hard to directly connect the content from the quizzes to our class discussions. This seems to be working.

Figure 5.6.   Reflection using voice recognition.

Analysis: This entry describes the environment of the classroom, but it also discusses technical considerations such as group work and connecting the quizzes to class activities. While this example may seem repetitious, it is included because it is the product of a VR program. I sent it via my iPad immediately after students left the classroom, enabling me to analyze my words more quickly and in a more real-time manner than if I went back to my office and wrote it down. While there were some glitches in terms of accuracy, the program was successful for this somewhat shorter journal entry.

In the situation presented next, I broke a rather large assignment into smaller assignments and had students hand these in; I proceeded to grade these in a purely formative manner. The journal reflection brings to the surface a concern of mine that had been popping up for some time now, namely, the practice of using rough drafts (formative assessment). In this situation, other concerns begin surfacing. Figure 5.7 contains the entry.

One of the things that came up as I was looking at the surveys was how good breaking things up [benchmarking/chunking an assignment] really helped them do the assignment. But something else came up. Only one person said it, but it's the idea of the formative part, how I wrote comments to help them improve it, and this goes back to something else that's been bugging me ... ummm ... How much do we really do? But it comes back to the conversations we've had lately, how much do we help them? How much extra help do we give them?

There is another issue, and umm ... for the time management study, there was more stress for me because what if I don't do a great job of giving them formative comments, then what? Now, they come back with the final assignment and I blast them? That just not right or ethical, but it takes so long to grade them. This comes back to two issues: (1) How much help do you really give them? (2) My own time management, do I have time to do more grading? Maybe, there is a third thing. Stress for me. Knowing you better grade them right and thoroughly, if you don't and the final draft comes back to you not as the best, and then blast them? Then you're really in trouble. Even though the kids really seem to like this, I really need to come with a plan. Maybe some research, talk to other teachers. How do they handle such things, time wise and ethically-wise? Maybe some research on students. I'm not happy with this. I've got to look at things differently, but I can't get started.

Figure 5.7.   Reflections on formative assignments.

Analysis: This not only brings up the core value or assumption of how much assistance to provide students, it brings up the issue of teacher time. At first this seems to be at the surface level, but the reflection does discuss the ethical dilemma of what could happen when one does not grade a formative assignment as thoroughly as possible.

5.4.2 A Graphical Tool With Narrative

The next focuses on the situation that while I use many Constructivist activities to deliver my courses, these activities do may take away time from course content. Let's look at the reflection in Figure 5.8.

As I prepare for my fall courses I have read over my previous reflections. One issue keeps popping up. I realize that am important issue is that of modeling my Constructivist activities in all of my classes. Am I spending too much time on these, and not spending enough time on core content of the course? Hmm ... This issue keeps popping up, so I need to revisit it.

Figure 5.8.   Reflection on Constructivist activities.

Analysis: This reflection summarizes a reoccurring issue that I wanted to look into with more detail. I decided to try another mode of reflection, the force field analysis sheet. This is a tool developed by Kurt Lewin (Sky-Mark, 2011) for examining the forces that are for analyzing change. One

Forces For	Score
Students like my constructivist activities	+5
I feel good I am modeling best practices	+4
Have activities ready to go for student teaching	+5
I do tie this in with assessment	+3
Reinforced by methods courses	+3
	20

Using Constructivist Student-Centered Activities

Forces Against	Score
Feeling a guilt for falling behind	-5
There are some of topics I need to cover	-5
Some topics must be added	-5
Some topics need more time	-5
Time taken away from assessment	-3
Topics that may be emphasized in other colleges	
	-23

Scoring this way shows that it may be time to do away with emphasizing Constructivist activities, but I really don't feel that way as yet. Even my Chair has made positive comments stating that the students like these activities. I need to reassess my numbers, maybe. Do I really need to feel that guilty? It isn't as if I'm not teaching, maybe I should add in points for the chair's comments. Looking at the numbers, it may be a case of doing some juggling. I have to create a curriculum committee, anyway – for State requirements, so I can work with these committee members, some of whom are practitioners to see what topics are priorities, which ones are not, and how much time? This committee may be the answer for looking at these questions. I need to create a new thinking scheme for dealing with this situation, and the committee for the state may be the answer.

Figure 5.9.   Narrative and visual tool.

applies a score to each force and then compares the totals. Figure 5.9 is my attempt at using this tool.

Analysis: This reflection using narrative and a visual tool (a force field analysis chart) is an example of using multiple modes for journaling. The entry focuses on the disequilibrium stemming from the process of using Constructivist activities taking away time from the content topics of Measurement and Evaluation. The low score on the force field analysis "forces" me to address the problem. Since I don't want to abandon the Constructionist approach, I need to consider ways to reduce the negative forces. My first reaction—very human!—is to fudge the scores (i.e., lower the first entry about my feelings of guilt). But that is a negative, and likely to be only temporary. I then consider more positive options for action. Specifically, the journal entry begins the transformation process by pointing out the possibility of still using Constructivist activities by doing some "juggling" through prioritizing topics and working with a committee to create a new scheme for this situation.

5.4.3 Cartoons

While I certainly am not an artist, tools are available that enable one to draw. This "cartoon" depicts my difficulty with determining the driving force of our curriculum at Saint Ethelreda. I make the reflection more powerful by combining it with a narrative.

Analysis: Combining two modes, the entry shown in Figure 5.10 uses an analysis of process and content to develop the question of what types of skills are the most important to emphasize. The disequilibrium brought out by the reflection is that of determining priorities, namely, what type of thinking is most important for students to learn? This question is at the heart of one's teaching persona. The use of the visual mode brings some important meanings to surface. The symbolizing of what really is important through the gas pumps demonstrates the belief that teaching and curriculum go nowhere without creating priorities. As a driver, do I choose regular or premium? What brand of gasoline is best for the car? As a teacher what thinking skills do I choose? "What brand" of thinking skills is best for students? The gasoline metaphor points to the fact that blending two gasoline products may result in a watered down product. The implication is that the combining of thinking skills would be ineffective, or not as effective as choosing one type of thinking skill. While this conclusion may not be true, it certainly merits consideration.

Standardized
Tests

Thinking Skills

Survival Skills-
teamwork,
note-taking, etc

Which Brand Drives
our Curriculum?

I have really struggled with coming up with a curriculum plan and guidelines for our curriculum mapping document. The bottom line is I can't determine what the foundation is, but" foundation" is the wrong word. Our curriculum is not a warehouse of "educationese"; rather it is like a race car that drives our students to success in the 21st century. What really is bugging me is what the driving force is? What is most important? Is it survival skills first, with those other skills just being taught as the result of teaching 21st century skills? Or is it reversed with the standardized tests or thinking skills first? Or is it a blend (like ethanol)? That really bothers me because that implies watering down. I really need to be more specific with my educational philosophy. While I might want to say all three, my work on the curriculum leads me to think that one must be the "fuel" for the curriculum.

Figure 5.10.   Cartoon and reflection.

5.5. Special Considerations: Using Artifacts

I now present another example from Saint Ethelreda, a handwritten note (Figure 5.11) that starts the transformation process by stating an emotional incoherence, followed by a question that leads to using artifacts for examining deeper issues.

I decided to reexamine some of the artifacts from my teaching at Saint Ethelreda. Figures 5.12, 5.13, and 5.14 are representative sample of the artifacts I randomly chose.

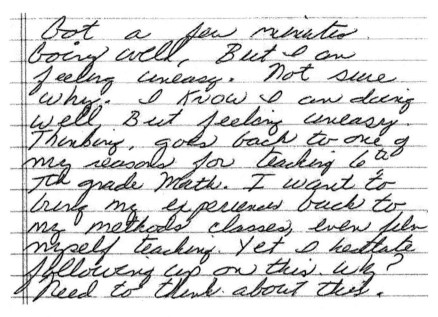

Figure 5.11. Journal entries showing emotional incoherence.

ARTIFACT 1

THE MINI MART PROBLEM

*NAME*_____

1. *You have gone to the mini mart and spent $23.89 on gas and you buy $11.21 of candy, about how much money will you spend? Do this by estimating. Discuss this in the space below.*

2. *Suppose gas is costs 2.95 per gal and you buy 10.05 gal. About how much money should you get back if all you have is two $20 bills? Discuss in the space below.*

Figure 5.12. Artifact 1: minimart problem.

ARTIFACT 2

Benedictine University and Saint Ethelreda Partnership
Spring 2011
Newspaper Article Summary Activity

1. *For the upcoming week's activity you will summarize the week's math topic, but you will NOT summarize it in the traditional format.*

2. *You must write a newspaper article that summarizes the important points of the week's <u>topic.</u> As a <u>minimum</u> you must have:*

   A. Headline
   B. Your names as the reporters
   C. The important terms, ideas
   D. The important
   E. Examples, diagrams
   F. Who, What, Where, When, Why

3. *This will be due on* _____

4. *To receive full credit you must:*

   A. Put in the form of a newspaper article
   B. Discuss the main ideas, important term
   C. Provide examples, diagrams
   D. Cover Who, What, Where, When, Why
   E. Write a reflection which:

   •*Examines the type of thinking you used in writing the newspaper article*

   •*How the thinking you used in writing the newspaper article differs from the thinking you use in doing homework or studying for a test or quiz*

   F.Hand in on time.

Figure 5.13.   Artifact 2: newspaper article exercise.

ARTIFACT 3

Saint Ethelreda/Benedictine University Partnership
THINKING SKILLS

1. *Check answer. Was it correct? Why or why not?*
2. *Check answer with partner. Did your partner do it differently?*
3. *What procedures should be followed?*
4. *Are there other ways to do the problem?*
5. *What do I know?*
6. *What do I need to do?*
7. *What do I still need to do?*
8. *Connect this problem to other ideas.*
9. *Use different words to describe your thinking.*

Figure 5.14.   Artifact 3: Thinking skills problem.

After these artifacts were created, I began the reflection process.Figure 5.15 presents my thoughts on these artifacts.

It became very evident what may be going on. Most of the artifacts I chose were Problem-Based Learning Situations (Problematics), curriculum documents, or lifelong skills. There were not any documents concerning curricular topics. I started to wonder if this was a trend. I looked over my material from the last couple of years, and for the most part, very few documents (mostly from this year) focused on specific curricular topics such as equivalent fractions, estimating sums, measuring, etc. The question is why? One reason may be that one of my goals was to bring PBL to the school, but it has been a few years, and I have not grown in another direction. I certainly could teach the mathematical skills needed to solve the Problematic, but until this year, hardly anything has been done in that direction. I wonder if I am afraid that I have forgotten how to do these types of things. I know I really jump at PBL activities and curriculum documents, But there is much more to consider such as topics from the curriculum. I haven't grown in that direction, and I wonder if I could learn more from the Saint Ethelreda teachers on how to teach such topics. This would help all parties grow. This comes down to developing a deeper relationship with my working partners and start sharing our individual goals and our strengths. It may be more about really building on our already strong relationship with each other, and using it to look more deeply how each partner can now contribute in different ways.

Figure 5.15.   Disequilibrium about problem-based activities.

Analysis: The handwritten note brings up the disequilibrium, which is then explored by using the artifacts to bring the real story to the surface. Focusing on process and content, the reflection looks for the underlying assumptions and relationships and starts the transformation process by creating a new mental filter. That filter is analyzing the relationship between me and the Saint Ethelreda teachers.

5.6 A Real-Time Reflection

My department is holding curriculum meetings to realign our curriculum. The note in Figure 5.16 brings to the surface the thoughts that have been coming to my mind during these meetings.

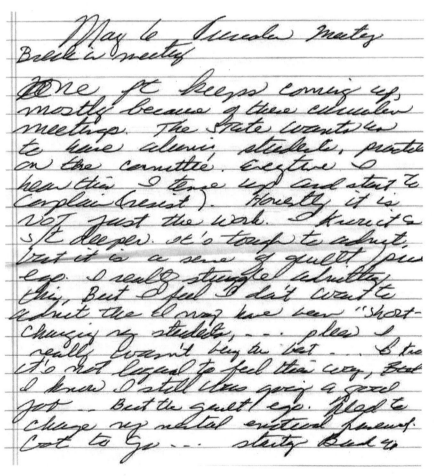

Figure 5.16.   Real-time journal entry.

Analysis: This handwritten note is important because it represents real-time data, whereas with reflections there is some lag time between the event and writing about that vent. Additionally, journal entries are often done when there is time to deliberately filter one's thoughts. In this situation, there was a limited time to put my thoughts on paper (a 10-minute break during a curriculum meeting), and even less time between these thoughts occurring and my writing of this note. Thus, this note has "real-time" significance.

The note brings to the surface a reoccurring uneasiness that I was not doing as much as possible for students at the time. This reflection illustrates an underlying cause or assumption for the disequilibrium. As the reflection indicates, my uneasiness might not make logical sense, yet it must be addressed. The reflection thus is the trigger for changing my expectations and creating a new cognitive and emotional scheme for interpreting my teaching situations.

5.7 Summary

We have examined one tool of teacher transformation: the journal. Teacher journaling can take many forms, such as handwritten, word-processed, audio, video, or a combination. Figure 5.17 summarizes our discussion so far.

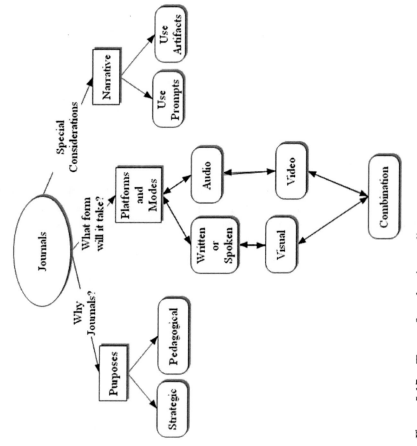

Figure 5.17. Types of teacher journaling.

CHAPTER 6

INTERACTIVE JOURNALS

Let's take a look at an effective way for applying one of our learning strategies, "Rattle Your Cage." That learning strategy directs us to create situations in which our present mental framework for processing experiences is inadequate. One way to do so is through interactive journaling—a reflective process in which one person creates a journal entry and the partner responds to it. The response may support the original writer, ask for an elaboration, or even challenge the ideas presented. The process is iterative and provides an opportunity to "rattle the cage."

First, we provide a rationale for interactive journaling. We then examine the potential disadvantages of interactive journals and present practices to address these disadvantages. The chapter cumulates with examples and an overarching framework.

6.1 Why Interactive Journals?

Interactive journals provide advantages that cannot be provided by individual journal entries. Roe and Stallman (1994) studied the dialogue and response journals of a graduate class of literacy educators. The dialogue journals required students to hand in their journal at the weekly class session, and these would be returned with instructor comments the next week. The journal response format required students to write weekly reflections, but these were not collected weekly. The results indicated that

Guide to Transforming Teaching Through Self-Inquiry, pp. 53–64

both formats were beneficial but that the dialogue format offered more in terms of collegial consultation, task engagement, and confirmation of ideas and feelings.

Interactive journals provide a platform for personalizing an educator's learning and for starting the process of changing one's teaching. Maloney and Campbell-Evans (2002) state that interactive journals provide a type of feedback that is "personal, specific and relevant" (p. 45). In this model, the feedback comes not in the form of specific tasks to do or specific answers but, rather, in the form of "possibilities for action" (p. 45). It is the initiation of an action plan that can begin the transformation process that is the focus of our book.

As a motivational tool, interactive journals can be an asset to the learning process. As Maloney and Campbell-Evans (2002) tell us, the feedback from university teachers "acted to focus their attention on progress and motivated them to continue" (p. 45).

Interactive journaling can benefit teachers whose learning styles are more reflective. As stated by York-Barr, Sommers, Ghere, and Montie (2001), these teachers then "have time to craft their questions or think about responses. For some, face-to-face interactions are difficult" (p. 71).

Interactive journaling also has advantages for the classroom. Besides providing a platform for students to view events from a different perspective, interactive journaling provides teachers a way of being more aware of classroom events (Maloney and Campbell-Evans, 2002). Additionally, by exchanging comments on a specific topic or lesson, teachers can clarify misunderstandings or motivate further study. In turn, teachers can gain a new perspective from the students. Moreover, teachers and students alike are able to discuss wider issues that develop over time. This type of interaction provides many opportunities for a deeper understanding of teaching.

6.2 Cautions to Consider

While interactive journal writing does offer several advantages, it also raises some concerns. Indeed, several studies have found that, instead of helping the teacher or student, interactive journals had the opposite effect. O'Connell and Dyment (2011) discuss these very points. They examine advantages and challenges of reflective journals, but these ideas can be applied to interactive journals. The challenges include gender issues, the issue of pleasing the instructor, and ethical issues. Hobbs (2007) notes that teachers may well feel that the process of critiquing entries and providing feedback actually implies that there is a preferred or standard way of writing journals.

More troublesome are matters of ethics and privacy that can be raised by interactive journaling. Ghaye (2007), in writing about reflective portfolios, claims that they introduced "a plethora of ethical issues" (p. 151). Included are such concepts as anonymity, privacy and dignity, confidentiality, interpersonal conflicts, and encroachments on personal liberty.

6.3 Addressing the Cautions and Building Trust

Since reflection is a key component to teacher improvement and transformation, it is of paramount importance to directly address these cautions. According to Ghaye (2007), ethics is about how we treat our fellow human beings. He presents five principles that can be used to guide the relational aspects of learning; in doing so he encourages teachers to show gratitude to the students for sharing their thoughts. Additionally, he emphasizes that no harm should be done to any of the participants in the sharing process and that participants should provide comments that will bring benefits. The following journal prompts address these concepts:

- Yes, I agree. I have done something like that in my teaching.
- Thanks for bringing this point up; I have forgotten about it.
- I like these ideas [specifically names them, and now you have me thinking in a different direction.
- Interesting entry, tell me more, if you want. Or if you don't feel comfortable with doing this, could you respond to the following …
- You have the right idea, and don't give up. I would suggest keeping with this strategy, and maybe try …

An overarching trait that will help in overcoming the potential obstacles with interactive journals is *trustworthiness*. In discussing the building of trust, Brewster (2003) stated that trustworthiness is judged according to the facets of benevolence, reliability, competence, honesty, and openness. He believes that the "willingness to trust one another is based upon the other party's actions and their perceptions of one another's intentions, competence, and integrity" (p. 6) and that trustworthiness increases with interaction over time.

The actions of creating trust can take the following form:

- as a teacher, coteaching with a fellow teacher;
- as a teacher, "swapping" classes;
- as a teacher, using ideas from another teacher and sharing the results of this with the teacher;

- as a person conducting professional development, coteaching with participants;
- as a person conducting professional development, helping grade papers;
- as a person conducting professional development, attending open house and parent meetings;
- as a person conducting professional development, attending as many teacher meetings as possible;
- as a university teacher, using student ideas in one's own teaching;
- as a university teacher, switching roles by joining a student group; and
- as a university teacher, maximizing the time before and after class to socialize with students.

6.4 Examples

The following examples are authentic interactive journal entries. The first three examples come from my Methods of Teaching Middle and Secondary School Mathematics class. This class consisted of undergraduate students seeking to teach mathematics and graduate students who were already certified in a content area and were seeking certification in mathematics. Each entry has a prompt from me, the student's response to the prompt, and my response to the student. The fourth entry is from a professional development course. The final example is part of an exchange of ideas between my colleague and me. In each case, I include an analysis of my response.

6.4.1 Example 1

The first example comes from a practicing teacher who was seeking certification in mathematics. In this example the student responded to the prompt concerning her changing view about teaching (see Figure 6.1).

Analysis: The prompt aligns with our metaphor of autonomy, asking students to examine their core values or personal values and theories. The student addresses core values by referring to teaching content and life skills. The entry "turns the kaleidoscope" by connecting to Maslow's theory (feeling safe). Moreover, by offering some suggestions such as sharing with other teachers, the response is acting as a catalyst for providing a

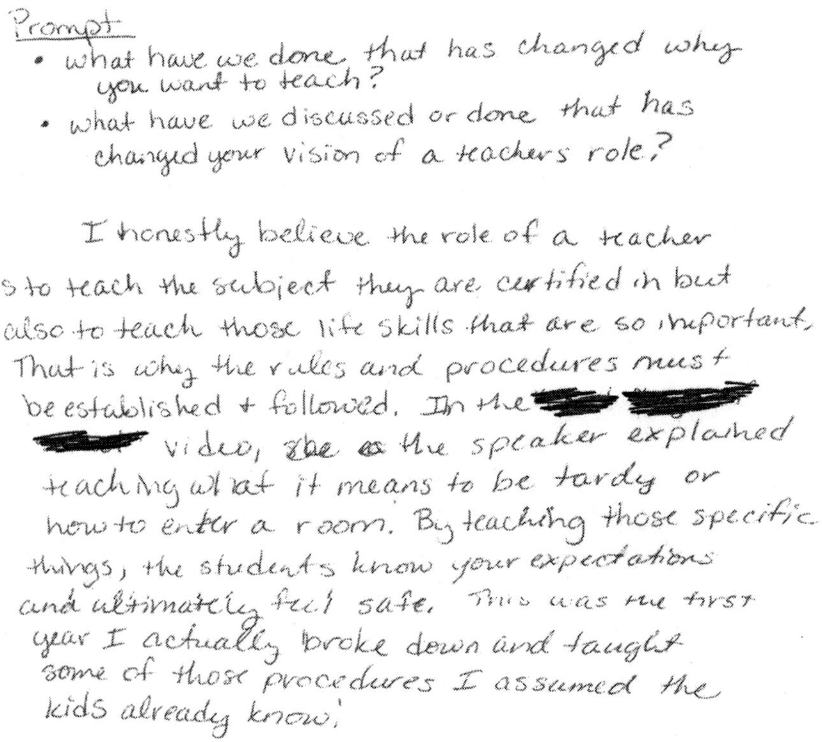

Prompt
- what have we done that has changed why you want to teach?
- what have we discussed or done that has changed your vision of a teachers role?

I honestly believe the role of a teacher is to teach the subject they are certified in but also to teach those life skills that are so important. That is why the rules and procedures must be established + followed. In the ▓▓▓ ▓▓▓ ▓▓▓ video, ~~she~~ ~~as~~ the speaker explained teaching what it means to be tardy or how to enter a room. By teaching those specific things, the students know your expectations and ultimately feel safe. This was the first year I actually broke down and taught some of those procedures I assumed the kids already know.

Figure 6.1.   Example 1 of prompt and student response.

benefit to other teachers, and also shows that the ideas of the journal writer have merit (see Figure 6.2). It could be beneficial as the next step to discuss with the student how this change in routine affected core values and the classroom environment.

6.4.2 Example 2

The second example also comes from my Methods of Teaching Middle and Secondary School Mathematics class. This student chose to respond to the prompt concerning the reason for wanting to teach (see Figure 6.3).

Analysis: This journal entry focuses on core values (autonomy/captain of your ship) by discussing how to help students and provide a positive role model. Also, this response aligns with Van Manen's third level of reflection, that of examining the moral and ethical elements of teaching. The

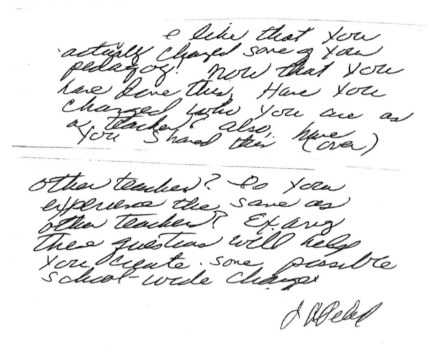

Figure 6.2.   Example 1 of teacher response to student.

phrase "You hit it on the head" shows that the responder appreciates the ideas presented in the journal. The response then "turns the kaleidoscope" by urging the student to turn his knowledge into action (see Figure 6.4).

6.4.3. Example 3

The third example provides another example of interactive journals; before you read the analysis of that response, see if you can determine how I might have better exploited the interactive journal process.

Analysis: The student entry (see Figure 6.5) represents Van Manen's first level of reflection, while it also "turns the kaleidoscope" by connecting the roles of the teacher to Maslow's theories. This entry also aligns with autonomy (captain of one's ship) by discussing a subjective interpretation of the roles of parents. The response is using autonomy by having the stu-

Prompt

What have we done, that has changed why You want to teach?

Answer

I think the more stories that I hear about a teacher helping a student in need makes me want to teach even more. Without teaching there is no way to know what the students will confront you with. I think it will be an awesome thing to do to help a student in need, or have a positive effect on their life. I realize now more then ever how many students are in need of a positive role model and I want to be that person for them.

Figure 6.3.   Example 2 of student response.

dent rank the importance of the different hats a teacher wears (core values) and also empowers the student to create an action plan (turn the kaleidoscope). Additionally, the process of ranking the different hats may actually change the core values or assumptions (see Figure 6.6).

Nevertheless, the instructor response misses an opportunity to help the student create a deeper understanding of the role of the teacher. The initial entry indicates that there are different types of parenting skills. The response journal should have contained a prompt asking for clarification and elaboration. Possible prompts follow:

- In what ways are the two types of parenting the same? Different?
- How do these different parenting roles align with your core values? Not align?
- How do these different roles influence your personal theories of teaching?
- Are you satisfied with your competence in the parenting skills needed by teachers?

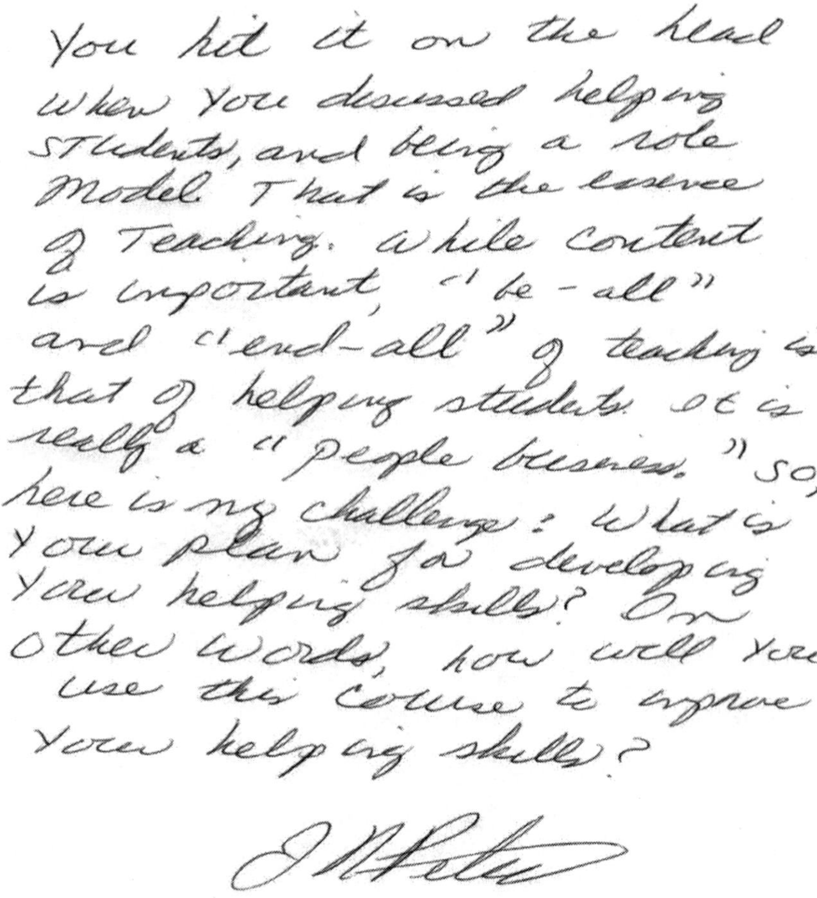

You hit it on the head when you discussed helping students, and being a role model. That is the essence of Teaching. While content is important, "be-all" and "end-all" of teaching is that of helping students. It is really a "people business." So, here is my challenge: What is your plan for developing your helping skills? In other words, how will you use this course to improve your helping skills?

Figure 6.4. Example 2 response of the teacher.

6.4.4 Example 4

The fourth example is from a 5-day professional development conference. Participants came in teams, with each team having definite goals and being assigned a facilitator. Each day team members would send an electronic journal entry to the facilitator. The facilitator would then respond. The following example comes from this process. Figure 6.7 contains the journal entry, and Figure 6.8 contains the response from the facilitator.

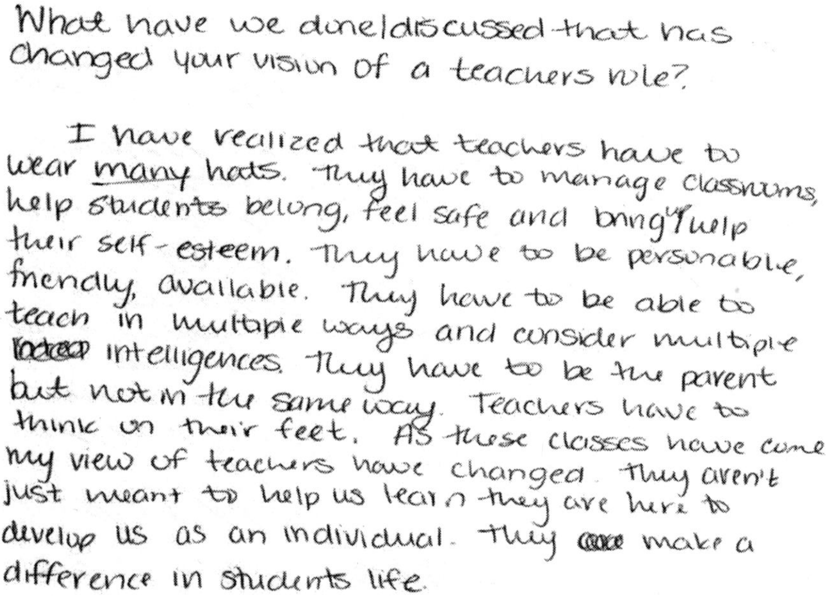

What have we done/discussed that has changed your vision of a teachers role?

I have realized that teachers have to wear many hats. They have to manage classrooms, help students belong, feel safe and bring/help their self-esteem. They have to be personable, friendly, available. They have to be able to teach in multiple ways and consider multiple intelligences. They have to be the parent but not in the same way. Teachers have to think on their feet. As these classes have come my view of teachers have changed. They aren't just meant to help us learn they are here to develop us as an individual. They make a difference in students life.

Figure 6.5.   Example 3 of student's response.

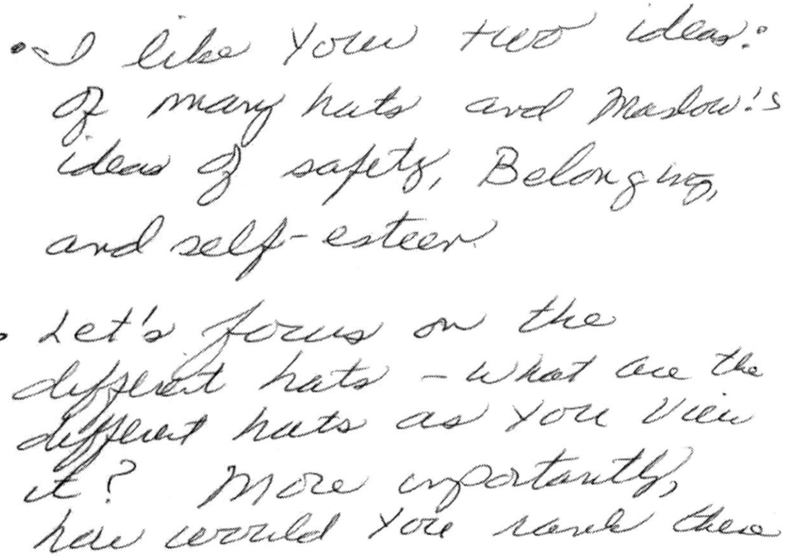

• I like your two ideas:
Of many hats and Maslow's
ideas of safety, Belonging,
and self-esteem

• Let's focus on the
different hats — What are the
different hats as you view
it? More importantly,
how would you rank these

(Figure continues on next page)

Figure 6.6.   Example 3 of teacher's response.

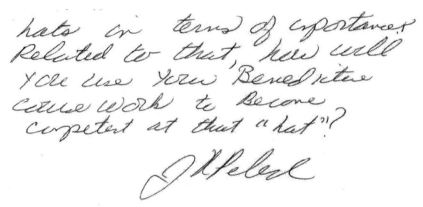

Figure 6.6.   (Continued).

I've had a great start to the conference today. I've already been thinking about chang-
ing my ways of thinking and how to better students' achievement. The elements we've
used so far in the process have helped the team's work mostly by focusing us. We now
know much better what we're actually trying to accomplish this week and we now also
have a good idea of how we are going to get there. Without a plan and a timeline, I
don't think we would be able to get as much as we'd like to finish.

   One insight that I've gained is the benefit of the teacher as a facilitator/guide. This
is one thing that I know I struggle with as a teacher. I have trouble allowing my stu-
dents enough freedom to be able to go out on their own to work on a task and for me
to simply guide them instead of instructing them. I have many fears about what
would/wouldn't be able to get done. Maybe the real problem is just that I don't know
how to help students learn on their own. The setup of the conference definitely enables
us to learn using Constructivist methods, but I don't know right now how I could use
the same principles in my classroom. One goal I have for next school year though is to
implement as many Constructivist elements as I can into my classroom and my teach-
ing. Although I struggle doing so, I definitely can see the benefit it would have on
students. I believe our rubric does a very thorough job defining our task for the week
and how we'll know if we're successful. I'm excited to really get working on our task
tomorrow!

Figure 6.7.   Example 4 of participant's note to facilitator.

I like the comments concerning students learning on their own—that is real teaching!
It is not a matter of standing back; rather it is a matter of picking your spots. By that
I mean asking questions to clarify what or why. It really is a matter of using questions
to clarify for yourself—you are now beginning the process of transformation.

   I also like the comments concerning applying elements in the classroom. We will
address this later on.

Figure 6.8.   Example 4 of facilitator's response.

Analysis: This journal entry is one of the earlier entries during the 5-day conference. The participant discusses changing her way of thinking and using conference elements in her daily teaching; these ideas are applications of "turn the kaleidoscope." The comments concerning students learning on their own and the teacher's role in this align with one's core values.

The response was intended to build trust in the participant, and this was done by encouraging the participant and offering suggestions.

6.4.5 Example 5

This fifth example comes from my work with Mrs. Lillie Pass at Saint Ethelreda School. We were exploring different strategies to increase reading comprehension. In this example students were filling out a graphic organizer about compound words. Figure 6.9 contains Lillie's entry.

Today Dr. Pelech and I had the students work on compound words. They had to create a descriptive definition, examples and nonexamples. I observed students using different words and ideas. It was surprising how the design of the graphic organizer influenced students. It was also surprising how some of the words used in the organizer were simple and some reflected a deep understanding of the idea. The discussions used by students carried over to when students use compound words in essays.

Figure 6.9.   Journal entry concerning reading comprehension strategies.

A portion of my response is in Figure 6.10.

I like how you say we can carry this over to essays. Applying or transferring over to new situations is a very important skill; I wonder if we can even discuss the idea of taking ideas form other subjects and transferring them to writing. By doing this I hope that students will see that we are modeling a process they can use for their entire lives.

Figure 6.10.   Response.

Analysis: The journal entry discusses the technical aspects of teaching and then begins the process of creating an action plan for transferring the concepts to that of writing an essay. The process of transferring ideas from one lesson to another can be an example of Van Manen's (1977) practical level of reflection, and if transfer is a core assumption or goal of one's teaching, then it can be considered as critical reflection. The response not only validates the importance of the original entry, it offers concrete suggestions and actions for extending the ideas contained in the original entry.

6.5 Summary

Interactive journals are another tool for the professional educator wishing to engage in self-inquiry. They make reflection intentional and visible; moreover, the feedback from another person provides opportunities for new perspectives, modifications of one's ideas, the validation of existing ideas, and the challenging of these ideas.

For interactive journals to be an effective tool of self-inquiry, participants must have total trust in each other in order to promote honest feelings and thoughts in journals. An environment of trust will enable the interactive journal process to be an effective avenue for self-inquiry.

CHAPTER 7

THE FOUNDATIONS
OF ACTION RESEARCH

So far we have examined the self-inquiry process and two important tools, the teacher journal and interactive journals. We now take the process one step further, moving from journal platforms into action research. In this chapter we look at the nature of action research, its components, and the prompts we can use to structure and implement action research in order to transform our teaching.

7.1 Action Research Versus Traditional Research

We will start with an exercise designed to help us create a working and meaningful definition of action research, which we consider a major part of self-inquiry and the process of creating knowledge and insight.

7.1.1 Exercise

The exercise presents five cases involving teacher activities. You are asked to put these five cases into two categories.

(A) A university professor goes into a classroom in a local school and studies the effects of a phonics program. She is interested in the

Guide to Transforming Teaching Through Self-Inquiry, pp. 65–75
Copyright © 2013 by Information Age Publishing

time it takes for students to learn to read. The researcher hypothesizes that the phonics group will be more efficient. Students are randomly assigned to two groups. One group is taught using the phonics approach, and the other is taught with another approach. At the end of the experiment the researcher compares the progress of each and then analyzes the results in terms of the hypothesis; the researcher looks at her results and determines if the results support the hypothesis. She uses statistics and statistical significance to determine if her hypothesis is correct. She has her research published in a professional journal and also presents it at a national conference.

(B) A teacher teaches a reading class. She is teaching it with a new phonics approach. During the week she observes her students and at the end of the week gives a test. The results indicate that the students kept getting the same question incorrect. She then consults the manual for another phonetic approach. She continues the next week teaching, but with that new method. While the results showed some improvement, she is not satisfied, and calls a friend who has used this approach. She then modifies her approach. The results from a test indicate that the modifications are effective. She also interviews students and conducts class discussions to get their perspective as to why a method works or does not work.

(C) A teacher is interested in what is the best preparation for improving test/quiz scores. For some quizzes students were given a study guide to complete on their own. For some quizzes they were just told and reminded to study for the quiz/test. The teacher then compared scores from the results, and made some adjustments. It became apparent that the majority of students needed more guidance from the teacher for improving test/quiz scores. This became evident from scores, from her observations, and from student surveys. The teacher then implemented interventions such as reviewing the study guide in class, modeling how to do problems from last year's tests, using/conducting graphic organizers, and teacher–led discussion of how to analyze the problems. The teacher also held classwide discussions with students concerning the results and methods for preparing for quizzes. The results of teacher observations, the surveys, and class discussions indicated that the best interventions were the following:

- Direct modeling of homework questions
- Direct modeling of questions from last year's tests
- Using graphic organizers

- Reviewing study guides in class
- Class discussion of an analysis of the problems.

These methods were then immediately implemented in the teacher's daily teaching.

(D) A university professor looks at different ways to conduct a teacher education methods course. One method she examines is that of using traditional methods of conducting a methods course. The second method is that of using Problem-Based Learning (PBL). After collecting data on the different methods during the year, the professor compares scores on the APT and uses "high-level" statistics to prove which method is better. The researcher publishes in a journal and presents at a conference.

(E) A university professor goes into a middle school once a week and coteaches math classes using "best practices." The regular teacher then uses these strategies during the week. The university professor comes back the next week and passes out surveys to the students to determine their reaction to the strategy. The professor and teacher look at the results and make changes to the strategy as needed. The university professor and the regular teacher try other techniques and the cycle continues. After three or four techniques have been examined, students are asked to fill out a survey to rank the strategies. The results are used to determine teaching strategies for the second semester.

While many categories are possible, here are the two categories my classes and I created.

- **Category 1:** Cases A and D. In these cases an outsider (university professor) conducts research in order to prove a theory or to statistically show that one method is better than the other. The researcher compares results in order to make a generalization. This category represents traditional research.
- **Category 2:** Cases B, C, and E. In these cases the research is done in a cyclical fashion and is done in the context of a teacher's daily teaching. The main purpose of the research is to improve teaching and student learning. Additionally, in these cases the stakeholders—teacher and students—are directly involved in the direction of the research, with the teacher being the researcher and the students providing input on data interpretation (class discussions and surveys) and future directions of the study. The cases in Category 2 are examples of action research.

7.1.2 Definition of Action Research

From the examples, can we formulate a definition of action research? Here the literature provides help. In discussing the purpose of action research, Hendricks (2009) states that action research is "for practitioners to investigate and improve their practices" (p. 3). Tomal (2010) defines it as "a systematic process of solving educational problems and making improvements" (p. 10). He expands on this definition by stating that the action researcher introduces "an appropriate intervention to collect and analyze data and to implement actions to address educational issues" (p. 11). Mills (2003) emphasizes the "research" aspect by stating, "Action research is any systematic inquiry conducted by teachers, researchers, principals, school counselors, or other stakeholders in the teaching/learning environment to gather information about how their particular schools work" (p. 5). He then explains the "action" part by noting that the goals of action research are to create positive changes in the school and on practice. Similarly, Costello (2003) stresses the transformational aspect: "Action is undertaken to understand, evaluate and *change* [emphasis added]" (p. 5).

Let us now create our own working definition of action research.

Action research is a systematic and cyclic research process done in the context of one's practices, conducted by a practitioner in conjunction with other stakeholders in order to improve one's own teaching and students' learning.

7.1.3 Importance of Action Research

Why is action research so important to educators? More specifically, why can't the research done by professional researchers (others) be the solution of a teacher's problems? Mills (2003), in discussing the goals and rationale for action research, cites the work of Kennedy (1997) to answer this question. Kennedy attributed the apparent failure of research to influence teaching to several factors, including the fact that much of the research was not relevant to practice and has not addressed questions that are important to teachers. Mills agrees. With regard to the relevance of research, he observes, "Either the problems investigated by researchers are not the problems really have, or the schools or classrooms in which the research was conducted are vastly different from their own school environments" (p. 12).

Let us now jump back to our discussion in Chapter 2 where we focused on what teachers do. Hunt (1976) told us that adapting to matters such as student moods, learning styles, and time of day represents the heart of teaching. Black and Halliwell (2000) pointed out that teaching is more than just applying theory, that it demands the juggling and taking account of multiple and opposing demands. It is this type of environment—the "context," as Mills calls it—in which teaching occurs, and it is in this type of environment that at least some educational research should occur, in order to be relevant to the classroom.

Another perspective on the rationale for action research emanates from higher education. Ernest Boyer (1990) identifies four types of scholarship at the university level: discovery, integration, application, and teaching. According to Boyer, the most effective type of scholarship involves asking questions such as "How can knowledge be applied to problems?" or "How can knowledge help individuals?" or "How can social problems themselves define platforms for scholarly inquiry?" This type of scholarship, applying knowledge to problems and using contextual problems themselves to define inquiry, aligns directly with action research. Action research, as a part of scholarly endeavor, is a staple for all educators.

7.2 Components of Action Research

Figure 7.1 illustrates the action research process as we use it in this book. As the figure shows, the process begins with emerging questions that we may have asked about our work. These questions do not appear out of nowhere. They come from the four metaphors and Constructivist principles presented earlier, from which teachers develop questions that address core values and assumptions. These emerging questions then evolve into research questions that help structure the action research process. The questions may represent problem areas or issues to be

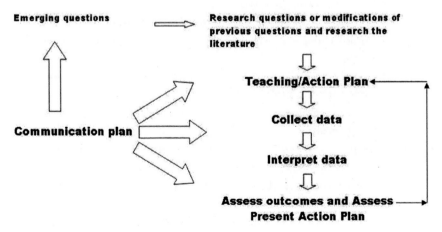

Figure 7.1.   Process of action research.

addressed, or they may represent teaching practices we wish to improve on or try in new settings. Like any researcher, the action researcher must then collect data. Almost anything in the classroom may serve as data. It may be test scores, student journals, and student work, the teacher's journal, anecdotal notes, formal and informal conversations with students, personal notes, and planning documents. The data is interpreted, and the outcomes are assessed: Did the plan accomplish what we wanted it to accomplish? This assessment may result in modifying the direction of the study or the research questions, with the cycle then repeating itself.

7.3 Prompts for Action Research

Since our version of teacher self-inquiry is driven by questioning, we provide here numerous prompts for the action research process.

7.3.1 Prompts for Emerging Questions, Research Questions, and Literature Search

Effective starting points for the action research process include anecdotal notes, notes and reports from previous studies, personal journals, and student artifacts. These can aid us in creating emerging questions. But an examination of the literature can also be helpful. As Tomal (2010) has noted, a literature review can provide benchmarking examples and identify the "best practices of other people and institutions" (p. 27). Here are some possible questions or prompts.

- What is bothering or intriguing me?
- What themes or concerns seem to be reoccurring?
- Do these themes represent satisfaction or dissatisfaction with my teaching?
- Do these themes or main concerns of the reflections represent my present teaching philosophy?
- Are there any emerging themes concerning certain theories? Concerning certain core values or assumptions?
- What has surprised me concerning emerging themes or concerns? Are there any explanations for this?
- Do the entries or artifacts represent a possible change in my philosophy or core values?
- Do I appear to be growing as a teacher or am I just maintaining the status quo?

- Do the school environment or school rules and procedures frequent my thinking?
- Am I speculating about a certain theory or procedure?
- Am I speculating at all?
- Do I need to reevaluate what is relevant for me?
- Does it seem as if my goals are changing without me realizing it?
- Do the same helping/hindering forces seem to be emerging?
- Are certain personal theories not working? Or working? Why or why not?
- What does the literature say about this situation and its solutions?
- Does the literature present methods and strategies that would help with this research?
- Do any of the themes from the literature confirm or align with my present beliefs or philosophy?
- Does the literature present strategies and theories that may result in transforming my teaching?
- What doesn't the literature examine?

7.3.2 Prompts for a Teaching/Action Plan

The action plan we create should include the critical factors to be addressed, specific teaching strategies to be used, pros and cons of the specific teaching strategy, theories that may be used, and any special resources required. Two other areas to be addressed by the action/teaching plan are a timeline and indicators of student learning. The following prompts will aid in developing a teaching/action plan:

- What is it that I am addressing? Is it a new innovation or a modification of what I already do?
- What are my goals for implementing this plan and these strategies?
- What theories will I be using with this strategy?
- Have I tried this strategy before? Do I need to rehearse this new strategy?
- Will I need to prepare my students for this new strategy? Will I need new resources?
- What problems do I anticipate may happen with this strategy?
- Will this new teaching strategy disrupt present routines?
- Will the implementation of a new strategy or modifications conflict with my philosophy? Will it conflict with the curriculum?

7.3.3 Prompts for Collecting Data

In action research, data collection is not a matter of gathering either quantitative or qualitative data. Rather, it is a matter of blending these two types of data together in order to develop a deeper understanding of the learning situation. Generally, quantitative data uses numbers to describe relationships, whereas qualitative data uses narrative to understand and convey the meaning of experiences. Qualitative data may include explanations on surveys, student and teacher journal entries, and transcripts from face-to-face interviews. Both types of data can and should be used together.

Let us consider the situation in which students fill out a Likert scale concerning their views on the effectiveness of a reading strategy (see Figure 7.2). Question 1 will generate quantitative data, while Question 2 will generate qualitative data that can provide information concerning the meanings for their responses in Question 1.

Following are some prompts that will help with data collection.

- What type of artifacts and data align with my teaching philosophy?
- What statistical tools and data align with my goals and outcomes?
- What resources or equipment do I need for collecting or generating data?
- What information will the statistical tools *not* be able to provide?
- Will the collection of data interfere with the daily routine of the class?

1. Look at the following statement. "This week's activity helped me learn mathematics." Please circle the response that describes how you feel.

O	O	O	O	O	O
1	2	3	4	5	6
Strongly dis-agree					Strongly agree

2. Look at your response from above. Write a few sentences to explain why you feel the way you do about the activity.

Figure 7.2.   Measuring student responses about the effectiveness of learning strategies.

7.3.4 Data Interpretation

Before we look at some prompts for interpreting data, let us briefly examine the term "validity." Many people interpret the term to refer to the accuracy of the data. For many educators, however, "validity" means "Did the instrument and data measure what it intended to measure?" And for action researchers, validity has yet a different meaning. Denzin and Lincoln (2003) address this point: "The core validity claim centers on the workability of the actual social change activity engaged in, and the test is whether or not the actual solution to the problem arrived at solves the problem" (p. 150). This view takes us back to the overall goal of action research, namely, the *solution of an educational problem*.

We can extend this concept of validity to include any matter pertaining to the improvement of student learning and improved teaching. For the action researcher, validity asks the question "How does the interpretation of the data help address the problem or goal?" Here are some prompts that will help us interpret data.

- Does the data represent a pattern? If so, does the pattern surprise me?
- What meaning do any patterns have for this research?
- Do any patterns conflict with my philosophy or expectations?
- Do any patterns conflict with any theories I follow?
- Are there themes? Do these themes align with my philosophy?
- Do these themes align with or contrast with my philosophy?
- Do different themes align with each other? Are different themes in opposition to each other?
- What teaching strategies can be derived from the data, including themes and patterns?
- How do different data sets compare or contrast with each other? What meaning does this comparison/contrast have for this study?
- What is the relationship between the quantitative and qualitative data?
- What doesn't the data tell me? What must I do to obtain this information?

7.3.5 Prompts for Assessing the Outcomes and the Action Plan

Assessing the outcomes and the action plan are pivotal actions for the action researcher. It is through such an assessment that subsequent decisions are made. The following prompts will get you started with this process.

- Does the interpretation of the data address the goals of this research? If not, what must be done differently?
- Do any steps in the action plan have to be changed? If so, why?
- Do any of the teaching strategies in the next steps of the action plan use any new theories or teaching practices?
- Do the next steps in the action plan represent a change in philosophy or established routines?
- What do I need to do to implement the next steps of the action plan?
- Am I emotionally and philosophically ready to implement the next step in the action plan?
- In what way does the next step in the action plan transform my teaching or classroom procedures?
- What are the helping or hindering forces for implementing the action plan?

7.3.6 Prompts for the Communication Plan

The purpose of the communication plan is to ensure that all stakeholders are kept in the loop concerning the planning, implementation, and results of the study. In many cases the communication is conducted via a two-way street. That is, the participants provide input that will be part of the results, and this input in turn affects the planning and implementation. Such feedback helps drive action research. Following are some prompts to help you reflect about your communication plan:

- Am I currently communicating with stakeholders?
- Do my current values include listening to the perspectives of others, including the implementation of their ideas?
- Have I consistently created a climate for communication in this class?
- What is my current communication plan?
- Am I willing to listen to others' perspective?
- What are my procedures for communicating with stakeholders?
- What type of vocabulary should be used?
- Do stakeholder perspectives contrast with mine? If so how? If so, how what procedures do I have to address this?

- Are stakeholders aware of the goals of the research? Are these goals meaningful to stakeholders?
- Do stakeholders believe that the data addresses the situation or goal of the research?
- Have stakeholders communicated how the research has been helping them?
- Have stakeholders communicate what sources are helping/hindering

7.4 Summary

Action research is a formalized, systematic process of teacher self-inquiry. Moreover, it is an important form of scholarship. This chapter has presented how action research is an essential tool for the educator who is interested in self-inquiry, and it has presented the framework for implementing action research. Now we are ready to look at some examples of action research.

CHAPTER 8

ACTION RESEARCH

Example From Middle School

As part of my work with Saint Ethelreda School in Chicago I work with
middle-school mathematics students and teachers. The example of action
research in this chapter emanates from this partnership and was carried
out in conjunction with sixth- and seventh-grade math classes during
spring 2011.[1] I acknowledge the support of Mrs. Lillie Pass, the middle-
school math teacher for this project, and the principal, Mrs. Denise
Spells, for her help and encouragement.

In discussing this example, I will use the components of the action
research process described in Chapter 7, provide examples of these
prompts, and then analyze these examples. This chapter looks at the
entire sequence of an action research project, starting with the emergence
of project questions, proceeding to the description of the project, and
concluding with an analysis of the project in terms of the principles and
foundations developed in previous chapters.

8.1 Overview of the Action Research Project

The action research project in this chapter follows our model from
Chapter 7. This research emerged from previous research and an exami-

Guide to Transforming Teaching Through Self-Inquiry, pp. 77–97
Copyright © 2013 by Information Age Publishing

nation of the literature. The process of the emerging question dates back to January 2008. A survey (Section 8.2) was given to students to determine their perspectives. The results of the survey were then used to drive an initial study, which was done during the 2008–2009 school year (Section 8.3). The results of this study were revisited in 2010, and an examination of the literature was conducted (Section 8.4). These results were used to drive the 2011 study (Section 8.5), which is the heart of this chapter.

8.2 Emerging Questions: The 2008 Survey

Denise Spells, Lillie Pass, and I determined that any action research or teacher professional development should start with student learning. A survey was distributed to students during January 2008 in order to determine student perspectives on how they learn. A portion of the written report of this pilot study is reproduced in Figure 8.1.

> *The results of the … pilot study indicate that middle school math students at Saint Ethelreda have metacognitive awareness at more of a descriptive level. They use general terms such as "helps you think" or "it helps me get it." They do not use phrases such as "I learn from others." Or "Working with other people gives me another perspective." Metacognitive awareness is essential to the learning; since students, teachers, administrators, and researchers must communicate to each other regarding student learning, it is essential that all concerned must have already constructed the concepts and linguistic categories necessary to communicate this learning. The study also indicates that Saint Ethelreda students do learn by reading their text and notes, asking another adult other than the teacher. However, the results of the study and informal, anecdotal conversations did not provide any in-depth into what exact activities help them learn or think. Thus, one resulting implication is that these students have not fully developed their metacognitive awareness (at their age, this may be understandable). These may be due to the framework of the pilot study.*

Figure 8.1.   Notes from the pilot study at Saint Ethelreda.

This note reflects some of our observations about student behavior as well as the students' own comments during formal and informal discussions. One interesting observation is that developing the "next level" of metacognition was important.

8.3 Emerging Questions: 2008–2009 Study

After many discussions based on the initial survey, Lillie and I decided to undertake two initiatives during the 2008–2009 school year. One was the introduction of Constructivist (student-centered) activities; the other initiative involved examining student perspectives on their learning (metacognition). To this end, we developed the preliminary plan presented in Figure 8.2.

The purpose of this study is to examine the metacognitive awareness of middle school students at Saint Ethelreda School. The research will be structured by the following questions:

1. *In the view of Saint Ethelreda middle-school math students, what Constructivist teaching strategies are most effective?*
2. *In the view of Saint Ethelreda Middle School math students, what are the reasons for the effectiveness of these strategies?*

Figure 8.2. Preliminary research questions.

In carrying out this plan, we partitioned our study into three 3-week cycles. Each cycle consisted of three different activities being introduced. Originally, these included cooperative learning activities, authentic writing activities (e.g., using math to write a flight plan or using geometry to help write a bid to sod and fence a lot), and Constructivist activities (e.g., toll booth exit passes). We concurrently introduced "mental math" tricks. These included "tricks" for multiplying by 11, or for multiplying by 25, or adding a string of numbers. At the end of the cycle, the students ranked each of the activities. Though the purpose of the research was to introduce Constructivist activities and to use these to measure student metacognition, mental math became a favorite of students. This is shown by the anecdotal note in Figure 8.3.

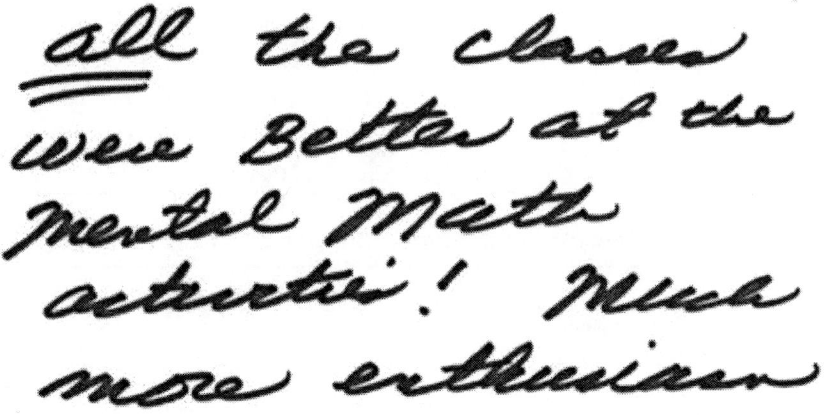
all the classes were Better at the mental Math activities! Much more enthusiasm

Figure 8.3. Comment on the success of mental math.

Motivated by the positive feelings of students toward mental math activities, we introduced these activities into the mix of the study during the second and third cycles. Mental math was ranked the most effective for both cycles. Note that the final ratings mirrored the individual rating given each activity.

Additionally, students were given an opportunity to explain their ratings. The objective was to enable us to analyze the types of phrases used. Student responses were categorized and coded in order to obtain a better understanding of student metacognition. The coding of these responses is given in Table 8.1. Table 8.2 displays the percentage of student responses in each category.

The data from Table 8.1 indicated that the majority of words or phrases used were of a general nature. Lillie and I decided to more formally discuss in math classes the types of activities that enable a person to think, with the intent that students would then use such activities.

Table 8.1. Coding of Student Responses

Category	Examples
Specific Cognitive Activities	• Share ideas with others
	• Use ideas other than my own
	• Compare other ideas
	• Put my math ideas into words
	• Discuss and agree on an answer
General Cognitive Activities	• Helps me remember
	• Think outside the box
	• Helps me get it
	• Helps me understand
Other	• I like Math
	• Tells us when to leave (the toll booth pass)
	• I don't like to read
	• It could be good or bad

Table 8.2. Percentage of Student Responses in Each Category

Category	Percentage of Students Using
Specific Cognitive Activities	20
General Cognitive Activities	64
Other	16

In the fall of 2010 Lillie and I revisited the question of the metacognition of students. We had already decided to emphasize cooperative learning activities, but we wanted a more formal foundation for our approach. I therefore undertook a literature search.

8.4 Emerging Questions: Examining the Literature

For action research, a literature search includes looking at past and present "best practices," looking at past and present theories concerning the topic, and looking at research designs. The following prompts from Chapter 7 were used:

- What themes evolved from the literature?
- Do any of the themes from the literature confirm or align with my present beliefs or philosophy?
- Does the literature present methods and strategies that would help with this research?
- Does the literature present strategies and theories that may result in transformation of one's teaching?
- What doesn't the literature study or examine?

Tables 8.3, 8.4, and 8.5 are transcribed versions of three of the notes I used to summarize the literature.

Examining the literature provides structure to the action research project. The literature search confirmed the efficacy of providing metacognitive training, which we wished to embed in our daily math instruction. The search also provided justification for the use of class time to directly discuss metacognition and gave us the incentive for creating a more formalized approach for teaching metacognition—including, for example, creating handouts on metacognition and formally writing metacognitive activities into lesson plans. Additionally, by identifying different levels of metacognition, the literature search provided the impetus for analyzing student responses in terms of general descriptive words or cognitive learning words.

8.5 Action Research Project: Spring 2011

During the spring of 2011 Lillie and I used action research to examine how our embedding discussions about metacognition into our mathematics classes would influence the types of metacognitive words used by stu-

Table 8.3.   Example 1 From the Literature

• Authors • Title • Journal	• Michalsky, T., Mevarech, Z.R., Haibi, L. • Elementary school children reading scientific texts: effects of meta-cognitive instruction • Journal of Educational Research, 102(5), 363-374, 2009.
• Summary • Findings	• Studied the effects of metacognition at different times of reading scientific texts—elementary students. • "Quasi-experimental"—treatment groups, control group • Treatment groups received metacognitive training at different phases of reading-before, during, after • Finding: Treatment group outperformed the control group • Finding: After reading metacognition training outperformed other groups
• What does the literature not cover or question?	• Not a naturalistic study • Student voice • Why metacognitive training helped (article brings this up) • Why the training after the reading was more effective • Effective for math
• Benefits to present action research project	• Confirms how metacognitive training can help with reading comprehension • Confirms the effect of embedding metacognitive training within content area • We will continue to do metacognitive activities and training within math lessons • Will use student voice—possibly answer "why this works"

dents. We also wanted to use these results to modify our teaching and curriculum. We formulated the following research questions for this action research project:

1. In the view of middle-school math students, what teaching strategies are most effective?

2. In the view of middle-school math students, what are the reasons for the effectiveness of these strategies?

3. Do students use cognitive learning words in their written and spoken explanations?

4. How can student metacognition guide and improve teaching?

8.5.1 Description of Activities

To investigate these research questions, Lillie and I established one 3-week cycle of three activities. Figure 8.4 is taken from the proposal we wrote to clarify our procedure.

Table 8.4. Example 2 From the Literature

• Author: • Title • Journal	• Romainville, Marc • Awareness of cognitive strategies: The relationship between university students' metacognition • Studies in Higher Education, 19(3), 359-366, 1994.
• Summary • Findings	• Study on first year university students • Examined the relationship between student metacognition and academic performance • Used structured interviews • Found that high achievers seem to be more aware of cognitive rules, and used these rules. • Found that higher achieving students described their cognitive strategy in terms of a complex sequence which used several relationships
• What does literature not cover or question?	• Did not study middle school or elementary students • The research specifically states that having lower achieving students adopt the metacognitive strategies of higher achieving students does not immediately improve the metacognition of lower achieving students. This may be due to the fact that metacognition, like all forms of knowledge, is constructed, and not transmitted. This aligns with our constructivist philosophy.
• Benefits to present action research project	• Shows that metacognition is a Constructivist activity, and that metacognition is not transmitted, but constructed. This aligns with our view of metacognition. • Provides a framework of metacognition—sequence of complex relationships. This can be used to analyze student metacognition. • Confirms use of metacognitive training • Did use interviews (student voice)-confirms the power of student voice. Student voice may be able to answer the question "why metacognition is effective in helping students learn."

Mrs. Pass and Dr. Pelech will guide students in a cooperative learning activity or in mental math. Students will participate in an activity, and then will be asked to complete a survey. At the end of the third cycle, students will rank the activities from all three cycles. The two teachers will then meet to analyze the results and to create plans for the next activity. It must be noted that during class activities both teachers will discuss the advantages of cooperative learning, and they also will discuss how one learns.

Figure 8.4.   Proposed 3-week cycle procedure.

For the first week of the cycle, students participated in a Think/Pair/Share activity; Lillie and I modified this activity to include students telling us what their partner said. We did this in order to help students improve their learning.

The second week's activity was mental math. We initially had wanted to do another cooperative learning activity, but we elected to do mental math because it had been received so favorably in the 2008–2009 school year.

Table 8.5.   Example 3 From the Literature

• Author: • Title • Journal	• Joseph, N. • Metacognition needed: Teaching middle and high school students to develop strategic learning skills • Preventing School Failure, 54(2), 99-103, 2010.
• Summary • Findings	• Summarizes research on self-reflective learning • States that most students need focused instruction and practice metacognitive skills • Students need to learn higher level metacognition skills as they go from one grade to another. • Provides suggestions for helping middle and high school teachers teach metacognitive skills-realistic advice and encouragement, class discussions about thinking
• What does literature not cover or question?	• Whether certain content areas need a special type of metacognition or metacognitive training-or do the same metacognitive skills cut across domain areas.
• Benefits to present action research project	• Confirms that student need formal training in this • This supports our decision to formally discuss metacognition • There are different levels of metacognition-this aligns with our desire to examine the types of words (general descriptive vs. cognitive learning words) students use.

Another cooperative learning activity, Partner Share Worksheet, was the focus of the third week. Figure 8.5 provides a portion of a Partner Share Worksheet.

This activity involves two partners. They both put their names on the sheet. Partner A does problem 1 and explains his reasoning to Partner B as he writes it down his work. If Partner A gets stuck, Partner B then

Name_____   Name _____

1) Solve for x and show all work   2) Solve for x and show all work

$3x - 5 = 22$ $5x + 11 = 49$

3) Solve for x and show all work   4) Solve for x and show all work

$4x + 6 = 26$ $9x - 5 = 67$

Figure 8.5.   Partner share worksheet.

coaches him. The teacher then discusses the work with the entire class. The roles are then reversed, with Partner A giving the paper to Partner B to solve problem 2.

8.5.2 Data Collection

At the end of each activity, we had the students fill out a survey, rating the activity on a scale of 1 to 6; see Figure 8.6.

The brevity of the survey was intentional. We wanted to make the research environment as natural as possible; doing so meant having the survey require a minimal amount of time to fill out.

At the end of the 3-week cycle, we also asked the students to fill out another survey. This one required them to rank the three activities; see Figure 8.7.

8.6 Interpreting Data, Assessing Outcomes, and Devising an Action Plan

We are now ready to see how the data was interpreted and how this influenced the action plan. The data and the action plan are printed with the permission of the *Journal for the Practical Application of Constructivist Theory*, which published our study under the title "An Action Research Approach to Examining the Metacognition of Middle School Mathematics Students."

Name_____   Date _____

Grade _____   Activity _____

1. Look at the following statement. "This week's activity helped me learn mathematics." Please circle the response that describes how you feel.

○	○	○	○	○	○
1	2	3	4	5	6
Strongly dis-agree					Strongly agree

2. Look at your response from above. Write a few sentences to explain why you feel the way you do about the activity.

Figure 8.6.   Student survey rating each activity.

Name_____   Date _____

Grade_____

Dr. Pelech has just reviewed the learning activities from the last three weeks. He has written their names on the board. Please rank these by writing the name of the activity in each blank. The first blank is for the activity that is the most effective for you. The second blank is for the second most effective activity. The third blank is for the activity that was the third most effective activity. Please feel free to explain your response in the space provided.

1.   Most Effective Activity for you. _____

2.   Second Most Effective Activity for you._____

3.   Third Most Effective Activity for you _____

Figure 8.7.   Student survey ranking the three activities.

8.6.1 Week One Data Interpretation and Action Plan

Table 8.6 presents student responses to the first question of the survey.

The results indicated that approximately 63% of respondents rated the Think/Pair/Share activity a 5 or 6. While this rating may seem high, approximately 21% of students rated it a 3 or lower.

The quantitative data tells us student ratings, but the narrative responses provide insights into the reasons and meanings for these ratings. Figure 8.8 provides a sample coding of student narratives.

Table 8.6.   Student Ratings for Think/Pair/Share

Response	Frequency	Percentage	Cumulative Percentage
1	2	8.3	8.3
2	0	0.0	8.3
3	3	12.5	20.8
4	3	12.5	33.3
5	7	29.2	62.5
6	9	37.5	100.0

One Learns from a Partner

- *It helped me learn because I can hear what my partner had to say about the lesson.*
- *I responded this way because I didn't know how to do it, but when my partner explained it to me in some order, I understood it.*
- *You get to share things with your partner.*
- *I chose 5 because you get to learn what other people learned.*
- *I agree because I might not know how to do the problem, but my partner would know.*
- *I learned about improper fractions from my partner.*
- *Because some people have different answers and we talk about them.*

A Partner Provides a Different Perspective

- *It tells me how other people think and the different ways to say or explain things.*
- *It helps me out because there was more than one answer so I learned how to do the problem in other ways.*

Disadvantages of Cooperative Learning

- *My partner did know the math himself.*
- *I already knew all of these things.*
- *I might not want to let my partner know that I think that it is hard, but I can't be afraid.*

Miscellaneous

- *It's fun and educational.*
- *I don't like fractions at all.*

Figure 8.8.   Sample student narrative responses on the Think/Pair/Share activity.

The first two categories of responses in Figure 8.8 indicate that students are using cognitive learning words. The coding category "Disadvantages of Cooperative Learning," by focusing on disadvantages, provides insights that could lead to a better implementation of cooperative learning.

To create a deeper understanding of student perspectives, we connected the quantitative and qualitative data to each other. Table 8.7 contains this data with all categories of narratives being represented.

Table 8.7 indicates that students ranking Think/Pair/Share a 5 or higher may have benefited from direction discussions about metacognition. This conclusion is based on their use of cognitive learning words. But one-third of the sixth grade said the activity was irrelevant, and 5 out of the 12 students in the seventh grade said it was irrelevant or negative.

Table 8.7.   Student Ratings and Narrative Responses by Grade Level

Sixth Grade		
Type of Narrative Response	*Rating*	*Number of Students*
One Learns from a Partner (or provides help)	5 or 6	3
A Partner Provides a Different Perspective	5 or 6	3
Learning as a Metaphor	6	1
Negative Response (I already know how to do the problem)	1	1
Irrelevant (Describes an algorithm or discusses irrelevant information)	4 or lower	4
Seventh Grade		
Type of Narrative Response	*Rating*	*Number of Students*
One Learns from a Partner (or provides help)	5 or 6	3
A Partner Provides a Different Perspective	5 or 6	3
Helps with Standardized Tests	4	1
Negative Response	Between 3 and 6	3
Irrelevant (Describes an algorithm or discusses irrelevant information)	Between 3 and 5	2

Naturally, such responses were a concern. Nevertheless, we decided to continue with cooperative learning activities as well as formal discussions about metacognition. Based on the interpretation of the quantitative and qualitative data, we created the action plan shown in Figure 8.9.

ACTION PLAN BASED ON WEEK 1 DATA

- *Continue using cooperative learning activities.*
- *Place increased emphasis on discussing with students the advantages of working cooperatively; this would include class discussions on the different advantages of cooperative learning, for example, how working with a partner provides new perspectives or how one can act as a cognitive coach for another.*

Figure 8.9.   Action plan based on Week 1 data.

8.6.2 Week 2 Data Interpretation and Action Plan

As noted, our plan was to continue with cooperative learning in order to keep the momentum going. The journal entry in Figure 8.10 reflects our students' response to that plan.

Obviously, the students wanted to do mental math activities. While we wanted to maintain control of the classroom and the curriculum, we felt that a few more minutes of the day on mental math would be beneficial and provide students with the feeling of autonomy. Although we have always used mental math in our daily activities, we decided to spend a few more minutes on it. Additionally, we deemphasized cooperative learning activities. The survey results are shown in Tables 8.8, 8.9, and 8.10.

The data in Table 8.8 indicates that the students overwhelmingly considered mental math more effective than the Think/Pair/Share activity: 81% rated the activity 5 or 6, compared with 67% for the earlier.

Tables 8.9 and 8.10 provide the qualitative data. The coding process that was used resulted in the categories shown by the two tables.

The data from the two tables indicates that students were using metacognition not merely as a descriptive tool but also as a tool to create theoretical categories that help in the process of understanding their own

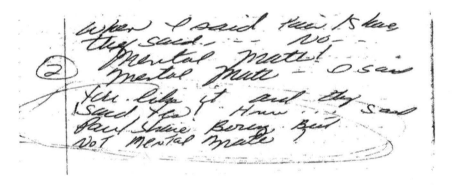

Figure 8.10.   Student response to cooperative learning vs. mental math exercises.

Table 8.8.   Student Ratings for Mental Math

Response	Frequency	Percent	Age	Cumulative Percent
1	0	0		0
2	1	4		4
3	1	4		8
4	0	0		8
5	7	29		37
6	15	63		100

thinking. This confirmed our belief that our discussions in class concerning metacognition were resulting in the refinement of student metacognition.

An emerging question was whether the limited use of cognitive learning words was the result that mental math was not of a Constructivist nature or that students were not able to apply their metacognitive skills to a particular and new situation.

We decided to continue doing mental math activities during the third cycle because we wished to examine more fully the student perspective on mental math as a tool for efficiency and as a second way to do math. The latter concept could lead to examining mental math as a thinking activity. At the same time, we decided to introduce a new cooperative learning activity, "The Partner Share Worksheet." While mental math still appeared popular, we wanted to go back to cooperative learning for two reasons. First, we wanted to make cooperative learning a staple of the curriculum. Second, we wished to gain more information concerning the use of cognitive learning words; we could then compare the number of cognitive learning words with the results from the first cycle. Additionally, we decided to interview students in order to gain more insight into their perspectives. The specific goals and guidelines for week 2 are shown by Figure 8.11.

ACTION PLAN BASED ON WEEK 2 DATA

- *Examine whether student responses for a new cooperative learning activity (Partner Share Worksheet) would differ from the first cycle.*
- *Examine how students rank the three activities.*
- *Examine whether students use more "cognitive processing" terms when explaining their ranking than in the first cycle.*
- *Determine whether students view mental math as a tool for efficiency or as a tool for thinking.*

Figure 8.11.   Action plan based on Week 2 data.

8.6.3 Week 3 Data Interpretation and Action Plan

During the third week, students engaged in the Partner Share activity, evaluated it as in the other 2 weeks, and then ranked the three activities.

Table 8.9.   Student Narrative Responses
for Mental Math—A Second Way to Do Math

- It helped me because it showed me a different way to add.
- I learned a different way to do math.
- I agree because it helps you learn good strategies.

Table 8.10. Student Narrative Responses
for Mental Math—Efficiency

- I learned to how to do math in my head quickly.
- Because it helps me do math in quick time.
- It is easy and stops you from counting on your fingers and guessing.
- It is faster and easier.
- It helps me sharpen my math skills.

Table 8.11 displays the results of students' ranking the Partner Share Worksheet.

A total of 78% of the students rated this activity 5 or 6, placing the Partner Share Worksheet second to mental math, but above Think/Pair/Share.

Since this was the end of the 3-week cycle, the students were asked to rank the three activities by most effective to least effective. Mental math ranked first, followed by the Partner Share Worksheet, and then by Think/Pair/Share. As shown in Table 8.12, the activity receiving the highest 3-week rating received the highest percentage for a 5 or 6 rating, and so on.

To gain a deeper understanding of student perceptions, we interviewed the students. Three major themes emerged from the interviews: (1) activities as tools for thinking, (2) the mechanics of thinking (cognitive learning words), and (3) the disadvantages of cooperative learning activities. Table 8.13 provides a sampling of these themes.

The student responses indicate that students were thinking about their thinking and experiences and that this thinking was beyond the descriptive level. The responses from all three categories indicate that students analyzed, compared, contrasted, and created categories for their different experiences. These responses provided evidence for the effectiveness of class discussions on metacognition. Some responses ("It helps me think more," "You think faster") labeled as "Tool for Thinking," however, sug-

Table 8.11. Student Ratings for Partner Share Worksheet

Response	Frequency	Percent	Cumulative Percent
1	0	0	0
2	0	0	0
3	0	0	0
4	5	22	22
5	7	30	52
6	11	48	100

Table 8.12. Weekly Ratings for the Three Activities

3-Week Ranking Activity	Cycle Rating a 5 or 6
Mental Math	92%
Partner Share Worksheet	78%
Think/Pair/Share	67%

Table 8.13. Sampling of Themes From Student Interviews

Tool for Thinking

- It helps me think more (Mental Math).
- You think faster (Mental Math).
- It helps me think about what I am doing (Mental Math).
- Helps me know something (Partner Share Worksheet).
- You find the weaknesses between you and your partner (Partner Share Worksheet).
- When I write it out I won't forget (Partner Share Worksheet).
- How I worked out the problem (Think/Pair /Share).
- What I was thinking about the problem (Think/Pair/Share).

Mechanics of Thinking (Cognitive Thinking Words)

- You learn different things from your partner (Partner Share Worksheet).
- My partner helps if I get stuck (Partner Share Worksheet).
- Show what we both know, try to make it better (Partner Share Worksheet).
- When I put it in my own language I understand (Think/Pair/Share).
- It helps me know what I do not understand about the problem (Think/Pair/Share).
- We paired together to see both of our ideas were the same or had the same comments about it (Think/Pair/Share).
- Two can help in a way teachers don't really understand (Think/Pair Share).
- Everybody get to hear different answers (Think/Pair/Share).

Disadvantages of Cooperative Learning Activities

- If you have a bad partner, it may not go well (Partner Worksheet).
- You feel like you don't need to explain, it's like something the teacher already explained (Partner Share Worksheet).
- If you do something wrong, they will get all mad (Partner Share Worksheet).
- Couldn't get to understand what partner said (Think/Pair/Share).
- When it gets time for me to ask them to repeat, it will be time for me to speak to my partner (Think/Pair/Share).
- Sometimes I don't like working with partners (Think/Pair/Share).

gest that the students still had not fully created an understanding of what it means to think or what activities empower them to think.

To make sure we were interpreting the results correctly, we directly asked the last group of interviewees to discuss what is meant by the term "thinking." We wanted to see whether participants would use cognitive thinking words. Table 8.14 displays some typical student responses.

**Table 8.14. Sampling of Themes
From Student Interviews—What is Thinking?**

- Show what we both know.
- I have to think about it first.
- Use your brain.
- To think means to use your brain to help you out.
- You think before you answer. You think before you talk, or you might say the wrong thing.
- Thinking is like ... when you think of how to do the problem ... think of the numbers.

The results in Table 8.14 confirmed what we had suspected: the students could recognize when they were thinking, but they had not yet fully understood what it meant to think.

8.7 Final Action Plan

We decided to create a two-pronged action plan, consisting of long-term goals and a short-term/intermediate goal. The short-term/intermediate goal was to be addressed during the remainder of the school year, and long-term goals would be introduced and addressed during the next three school years.

- *Short-term/immediate:* Conduct formal discussions in the two classes concerning what one does when one thinks.
- *Long-term:* (1) Start a formal process of examining how to address the weaknesses of cooperative learning; (2) examine how to integrate metacognition throughout the curriculum; and (3) examine the Constructivist nature of mental math and the cognitive activities involved in doing mental math.

8.7.1 Addressing the Short-Term/Intermediate Goal

Lillie and I decided to hold formal class discussions on student perceptions on what it means to think. We set aside an entire class period and portions of subsequent classes for this activity. We believed that by having students participate in discussions regarding thinking, they would be able to better understand what it means to think. These responses were used to create a student-produced "Thinking Skills Sheet" (Figure 8.12).

Saint Ethelreda/Benedictine University Partnership

Thinking Skills

1. *Check answer. Was it correct? Why or why not?*
2. *Check answer with partner. Did your partner do it differently?*
3. *What procedures should be followed?*
4. *Are there other ways to do the problem?*
5. *What do I know?*
6. *What do I need to do?*
7. *What do I still need to do?*
8. *Connect this problem to other ideas.*
9. *Use different words to describe your thinking.*

Figure 8.12.   Thinking skills sheet.

This sheet was used in the sixth-grade and seventh-grade math classes during the last days of the semester. The teachers "thought out loud" as they used the thinking sheets. Next, the teachers guided the students in their use of the thinking sheets. Students readily and enthusiastically used the sheets, and teacher observations indicated that the sheets were instrumental in guiding student thinking.

8.7.2 Applying the Thinking Sheets to Another Field of Study

For the fall of 2012, Lillie added language arts to her teaching load. Taking the initiative, she analyzed the thinking sheet and modified it so her eighth-grade language arts students could use it (Figure 8.13).

Saint Ethelreda/Benedictine University Partnership

Thinking for Writing 2011-2012 School Year

Mrs. Pass and Dr. Pelech

1. *What procedures should be followed?*
2. *What do I know about what should be written?*
3. *What don't I know about the topic? What must I do to learn this?*
4. *What other ideas can I connect to the topic? Can I connect personal experiences to the topic? Can I connect other subject areas to this topic?*
5. *What other strategies or perspectives can I use?*
6. *What have I written that has surprised me? Should I expand on this?*
7. *Did my partner write it differently? Can I incorporate any of my partner's ideas into my writing?*

8.   *What other words can I use in this essay?*

9.   *Are there other ways to write this essay?*

10. *After the revision, what can I still do? What do I still need to do?*

Figure 8.13.   Modified thinking sheet for language arts.

Since these eighth-grade students were part of the study from the 2010–2011 school year, they responded enthusiastically to using these sheets. Teacher observations indicated that students were using these sheets effectively.

8.8 Communication Plan

An important process during action research is implementing a communication plan throughout the project. As illustrated in Chapter 7, communication with stakeholders is embedded throughout action research. In this action research project we communicated continuously with students. We formally discussed with students the nature of metacognition, metacognition activities, and mental math; additionally, we discussed the survey results with students and used class discussion to expand on survey results.

While communication with participants (students in this case) is vital, we need to discuss another group of stakeholders: the parents. Since parents must sign a consent form and are responsible for their children, they are certainly stakeholders in this process. Communicating with them is critical, and such communication requires using a vocabulary and framework that they can understand. Another stakeholder, related to parents, is the administration. Since the principal has overall responsibility for the school, we were careful to seek the principal's approval and involvement. To this end, we drafted a letter to be sent to parents, and we then sent it to the principal for her approval and input. Figure 8.14 contains the letter that was sent to parents, with our principal's approval, explaining our action research project. (Note that although we reproduce the letter here, it was sent to the parents *before* Lillie and I entered the phase of examining student perceptions concerning what it means to think.)

8.9 Summary: Action Research and the Foundations of Teacher Self-Inquiry

Let us look at how our action research from this chapter aligns with our foundations of teacher self-inquiry. The foundations presented by Chapter 3 included phenomenology, turning knowledge into action, transformation, asking questions, and Constructivism. Our action research project aligns nicely with phenomenology, which studies the experiences of people and the meaning of an experience as they experienced it. In our case

Benedictine University/Saint Ethelreda School Partnership

ACTION RESEARCH SPRING 2011

Benedictine University educators are **effective practitioners**, committed to **scholarship, lifelong inquiry, leadership** and **social responsibility**.

To: Parents and Students

From: Dr. Pelech and Mrs. Pass

We would like to take this opportunity to thank you for participating in our Action Research Project. This project focuses on student perceptions of the effectiveness of different activities. Approximately each week students will rate the effectiveness of each activity; at the end of three weeks the students will rank each activity.

We recently finished the first phase of this project and the results indicated that students like mental math the best. The results also provide insights into how students view thinking, and this includes thinking as the checking of one's ideas and answers, and thinking as an activity done by oneself and in cooperation with others.

Our goal for the second phase is to expand our definition of thinking to include that of incorporating different perspectives and expressing our thinking in different modes. We will also explore making working with a partner a more efficient process.

Again, thank you for your cooperation and please feel free to contact us with any questions.

James Pelech, Ed.D.

Lillie Pass

Figure 8.14.   Letter sent to parents with principal's approval.

the research examined student perceptions of their experience of cooperative learning activities and mental math in real time. The concept of turning knowledge into action is seen throughout this project. Each inter-pretation of the data resulted in a plan for the next cycle. The knowledge resulting from the interpretation of data drove the next cycle's action plan and was seen in the final action plan, resulting in curriculum changes and new classroom practices.

Two of our foundational blocks, critical reflection and personal trans-formation, align nicely with our research. Critical reflection examines our previously held assumptions or core values, including examining prac-tices thought to be beneficial to students that may actually be hindering student learning. Personal transformation occurs when we use critical reflection to examine our practice and create a plan for change based on those changes. One of our basic beliefs was that students would automati-cally benefit from cooperative learning activities; the assumption underly-ing this was that students were cognitively and emotionally ready for cooperative learning. This action research project enabled Lillie and me to modify this assumption; both of us now believe that a teacher must examine "bridging" students so that they are cognitively and emotionally ready for cooperative learning.

Another transformation to our teaching was motivated by the role of metacognition. Previously, metacognition had been "something we did." Through this research project, however, metacognition emerged as a core value. Metacognition has now emerged as a *necessary element* to all learn-ing activities. Lillie and I now use metacognitive activities as vital parts of our teaching.

Asking questions and the principles of Constructivism were the driving forces of our action research. Using results of previous surveys and a pilot study (prior knowledge), Lillie and I created the research questions for this study. The interpretation of data in this project involved "turning the kaleidoscope" through coding, creating possible explanations and per-sonal theories, and finding personal relevance—activities that resulted in new action plans.

NOTE

1.   Published in the Summer 2012 issue of the *Journal for the Practical Applica-tion of Constructivism in Education*.

CHAPTER 9

PROFESSIONAL DEVELOPMENT

I know that many of us yawn when we hear the word "professional development." But using our foundations, principles, and prompts, I believe we can develop an effective approach to professional development. Before we do that, however, let's make sure that professional development is a viable instrument of teacher self-inquiry.

9.1 Professional Development, Student Learning, and Teacher Improvement

A teacher has one overriding purpose, and that is to help students learn. Let's examine how others have argued that this purpose is best achieved.

The discussion in Chapter 2 presented evidence strongly indicating that the most important variable in student learning is the teacher. Indeed, Mendler (2012) confirms this. In discussing the emphasis on research-based teaching methods, he states that "little of what is emphasized actually connects to great teaching and learning" (p. 2). He continues by citing the work of Goodlad (1994), who found that the effectiveness of the teacher was the only factor increasing student learning.

Let's look at some specific cases. Johnson and Fargo (2010) conducted a longitudinal study of science teachers at the middle-school level. Their results indicated that professional development not only improved teacher practice, it also improved student achievement. In another study that same year, the impact of embedded professional learning for mathematics teachers at two contrasting districts in Canada was examined by Bruce, Esmonde, Ross, Dookie, and Beatty (2010). Participants met in 2-day sessions on six occasions. During this time they created student learning goals, coplanned a lesson, and then cotaught or observed the lesson. The study demonstrated that collaborative and classroom-embedded programs lead to improvement in student achievement.

It seems logical to assert that improving the teaching ability of the teacher will improve the learning of students. On the other hand, some research concerning professional development and student learning and achievement leaves room for caution. In particular, Guskey and Yoon (2009) reported on a project carried out by the American Institutes for Research in which 1,300 studies were analyzed for the effect of professional development on student learning outcomes. And while teacher workshops or summer institutes were found to have a positive effect on student learning, only nine of these studies met the criteria of credible evidence set down by the What Works Clearinghouse (an arm of the U.S. Department of Education). The Clearinghouse reported on a study that examined the effect of professional development on reading instruction and achievement. The results indicated that the effect sizes of 0.03 to 0.08 were not significant. In a review of a second study, which examined seventh graders' knowledge of rational numbers when their teachers participated in professional development activities, the results indicated that professional development did not have an impact on student learning. Moreover, in examining the follow-up study the Clearinghouse's review concluded that, while participating teachers did engage in more activities per hour that enabled students to think, there was no statistical difference from results with control schools.

These latter studies should not be perceived as reasons for not implementing professional development. Rather, they should be perceived as challenges to all educators to design valid and rigorous instruments to ensure the effectiveness of program development as seen in the studies of Johnson and Fargo (2010) and Bruce and colleagues, 2010.

9.2 Approaches to Effective Professional Development

Presented in this section are five sets of prompts—or questions—that we as teachers can use for our professional development. While some of these prompts may overlap, our purpose is to build a conceptual foundation for our system of teacher self-inquiry.

9.2.1 Student Learning

Let us remind ourselves—however obvious it may seem—that the focal point of educational activities must be student learning, not teaching. Bellanca (2009) writes, "A school's professional development needs assessment is most helpful to all if it focuses on *student learning needs* [emphasis added]" (p. 16). This leads us to our first prompts:

- What student learning needs must be addressed at this time?
- How convinced am I that this initiative will help students learn?

9.2.2 Building Relationships

Professional development is about learning how to improve teaching and, hence, student learning. Initially, then, let us look at some ideas regarding how to facilitate learning.

Rogers (1969) believes that "the facilitation of significant learning rests upon certain attitudinal qualities which exist in the personal *relationship* [emphasis added] between the facilitator and the learner" (p. 106). For Rogers, building relationships involves highly regarding others and their ideas, establishing trust, and creating a sense of empathetic understanding.

Another practical method of building relationships is to make the participants in the professional development scenario feel valued. In discussing leadership, Cohen (1990) says, "If you want people to follow you, make them feel important" (p. 32). This concept blends with Rogers' idea of highly regarding other people and their ideas.

Cohen presents one reason for building relationships: getting followers. Another reason is presented by Conant and Norgaard (2011). Using as a model the Campbell Soup Company, they show the importance of inspiring trust: "Campbell's leaders would need to gain the trust of the employees before they could expect the employees to volunteer their best ideas and energy" (p. 52).

Whether you are leading a professional development initiative or participating as a member of a team, developing relationships is a key activity. The following prompts will help you build effective relationships:

- How can I make other people feel important?
- How can I show other people that I hold them in high regard?
- How can I develop a trusting relationship with other people?
- What can I do to develop empathy? What can I do to "walk a mile" in other people's shoes?

- What other teachers should be involved in this undertaking or would be interested? Do they have the same core values as I do?
- How can this new change positively influence the rest of the school?

9.2.3 The Adult Learner

Our Constructivist orientation to self-inquiry enables us to look at how teachers, as adult learners, may bring a special orientation to learning.

Knowles (1978) presents four assumptions concerning the adult learner. The first assumption is that the adult learner is a self-directed learner; according to Knowles; this includes "a deep psychological need" (p. 56). The second assumption Knowles discusses is the importance of experience in adult learning. As we mature, we depend less on having knowledge transmitted to us and more on learning through personal experience. The third assumption deals with the learning needs of adult learners. Younger students are deemed ready to learn based on their biological and academic development. Knowles reminds us that as we mature, our readiness to learn "is increasingly the product of the developmental tasks required for the performance of [our] evolving social roles" (p. 57). One's orientation to learning changes as one matures. Children will have a subject-centered orientation to their learning, while "adults tend to have a problem-centered orientation to learning" (p. 58). In other words, adults will come to professional development because of a problem that they are experiencing or because they feel that they need to improve in an area.

Given the characteristics of the adult learner, we can identify the following prompts:

- What do I need to improve on in order to help my students learn? What immediate problem do I need to solve?
- Is there a specific area in which I need to improve? Is there an aspect of my personal teaching theory with which I am not happy?
- Can I use this new idea in other areas of my teaching?
- How do we know that we need this change?
- What personal experience can I use to help solve this problem? Can what I used in a different content or context be used for these new student needs?

9.2.4 Autonomy, Vision, and Meaning

A first step in learning is wanting to learn. How, then, can we as teachers motivate our students to want to learn? In discussing how to get people to give their best, Conant and Norgaard (2011) writes that it is not about what personally excites us, but rather "it is about what makes *the other people* [emphasis added] engage wholeheartedly" (p. 64). If we agree with Conant and Norgaard, we might well need some professional development to help us reflect on our aims and actions and then experiment with them.

Knight (2007) defines this activity as *praxis*. According to Knight, praxis enables teachers to "have a chance to explore, prod, stretch, and recreate whatever they are studying—for example, really consider how they teach, really learn a new approach, and then reconsider their teaching practices, and reshape the new approach" (p. 49). Knight's vision of praxis implies autonomous educators who are continuously reflecting on and revising their teaching based on their experiences.

The business world is rapidly accepting the premise of the importance of workers creating meaning. Fullan (2008) examined companies classified as "maverick" and found that these companies "select and cultivate people who can find meaning and are seeking experiences that contribute to their own development and fulfillment" (p. 45). Another example from the business environment comes from the ideas of Sisodia, Wolfe, and Sheth (2007). In discussing the "Age of Transcendence" they write that the term denotes "a fact supported by numerous consumer surveys [showing] that people are increasingly looking for higher meaning in their lives, rather than simply looking to add to the store of the things they own" (p. 4).

Of course, as teachers we are dedicated to enabling our students to create their own meaning. This is true whether we are teaching "traditional-aged" students or adult learners. Effective professional development empowers educators to use or increase their autonomy by creating and modifying a vision of meaningful practice. Let's look at some prompts.

- Do I need to change my vision? Why?
- Does the change or new initiative align with or modify my core values?
- What meaning does this change or problem have for my teaching?
- How does this new initiative change my role as a teacher? Will this be a positive or a negative? Is there significant meaning for this new role?
- Do my core values help or hinder me in creating meaning for my practice?

9.2.5 Contextual Learning and Action Plan

As adult learners, in this case educators, we are concerned with practical, immediate problems. This implies that we must use new knowledge in the context of our own practice.

Fullan (2008) states that one "can achieve consistency and innovation only through deep and consistent *learning in context* [emphasis added]" (p. 86). In discussing the research that supports professional development, Darling-Hammond and Richardson (2009) state that teachers must acquire new knowledge, apply it, and then reflect on it with other teachers. Extending the concept of contextual learning to the concept of the process of change, Fogarty and Pete (2007), in discussing the research of Guskey (2000), write that teachers will "believe differently only after trying some things in the classroom and seeing positive changes in student achievement with their own eyes" (p. 4). This idea is reflected in Bellanca's (2009) concept of transfer, which he describes as a consciously planned result (p. 39). The phrase "planned result" is important to us. To transform our teaching, we must transfer or apply a new idea to our teaching and then reflect on the results and subsequent actions. Such a process requires a great deal of planning. Below are some prompts that align with contextual learning and an action plan.

- What is my action plan for implementing the change?
- What new or revised materials will I have to use?
- How will be teaching strategies be modified? Does this align with my core values, or does this modify my underlying teaching assumptions?
- How difficult will this change be in terms of time, materials, and procedures?
- What does this change sound and look like in my practice?
- How will I measure success in terms of student outcomes and learning?
- What will be the metrics/measurement instruments for restructuring the action plan or my overall teaching /core values?

9.3 Instruments for Effective Professional Development

Armed with these prompts, let us now consider tools that can translate these prompts into action and effective professional development. I am grateful to Don Mesibov and Pat Flynn of The Institute for Learning Centered Education for their ideas and expertise on developing tools for professional development; their ideas are the foundations for the seven tools we will examine:

- Guidelines for Coexperiencing
- Protocols

- Goals and Tasks Worksheet
- Graphic Organizer
- Assessment Plan: Outcomes and Evidence
- Project Rubric
- Action Plan

We will briefly look at how they translate our prompts into action. The examples come from my work at Saint Ethelreda School in Chicago.

9.3.1 Guidelines for Coexperiencing

The term "coexperiencing" is a key element of our system for professional development. If you are fortunate enough to be facilitating in-service or professional development on a continual basis for a school, then this is a key element for your effectiveness. While we all have said something like "I know how you feel," it is imperative for our system that you *actually* know how the teachers you are working with feel and think. Let's look at this in more detail.

Our earlier discussion on relationships emphasized the importance of building trust, having empathy, and making the other person feel important. If we look at our closest relationships in life, we will see that many of them were the result of having the same types of experiences or experiencing the same phenomena with another person. It may be one's college roommate or a coworker from one's first job. While coexperiencing, then, may seem to be the same as the concept of "coteaching," it must go deeper and be more encompassing than that—to create real and deep relationships we must "walk a mile in the others' shoes." Note the plural "others." In delivering professional development, it is of the utmost importance to live the life of those with whom you are working: not just your coteacher, but also other teachers, parents, students—the entire school. The "Guidelines for coexperiencing" in Figure 9.1 provide the prompts.

1. *Have I started the process of coteaching?*
2. *Does my coteaching include coplanning? Does my coteaching include all activities, including grading papers?*
3. *Have I used ideas from my coteaching partner?*
4. *Have I empowered my coteaching partner to initiate ideas?*
5. *Have I worked as hard implementing my coteaching partner's ideas as I do my own?*
6. *Have I empowered my coteaching partner to initiate research ideas?*
7. *Do I eat lunch with the teachers?*

8. *Do I eat lunch with students?*
9. *Do I share planning time with the teachers?*
10. *Do I go to Open House and Parent/Teachers Conference?*
11. *Do I go to school functions?*
12. *Do I interact with students and teachers before and after school?*

Figure 9.1.   Guidelines for coexperiencing.

9.3.2 Protocol

In teaching, protocols refer to administrative and "in-house" procedures for conducting an activity. While they need not have a formal structure as they do in political situations, they still are written down and agreed upon by the participants. But one-size protocols do not exist (or if they do, they are probably not effective). Rather, the form and content of the teaching protocol are dependent on the development and needs of the cohabiting relationship. Figure 9.2 is an example.

SAINT ETHELREDA SCHOOL AND BENEDICTINE UNIVERSITY PARTNERSHIP

1. *The overall goal for this year is to create a repertoire of teaching activities which Mrs. Pass can use to teach literature to 7th grade students at Saint Ethelreda School. This will include a portfolio/file of these activities.*
2. *Mrs. Pass and Dr. Pelech will create a system of assessment tools for evaluating the effectiveness of these activities.*
3. *Dr. Pelech will be observing and teaching in the 7th grade literature class*
4. *Dr. Pelech will teach literature classes while modeling "best practices." Mrs. Pass will observe, with the following occurring:*
    o   *Mrs. Pass will also participate in teaching the class*
    o   *Mrs. Pass will also make sure students are engaged by using MBWA*
    o   *Mrs. Pass will talk with Dr. Pelech concerning these activities—with informal and formally scheduled times*
    o   *Mrs. Pass will implement these techniques during the week*
    o   *During the week Dr. Pelech and Mrs. Pass will have formal discussions on these and will work together on future activities, and this includes planning and correcting papers.*
    o   *These roles of teaching/modeling and observing will be reversed not only during a lesson, but also to start a lesson. There will be lessons where Mrs. Pass starts out the lesson modeling her version of "best practices."*
    o   *Mrs. Pass and Dr. Pelech will keep a portfolio/file of all activities*
5. *Mrs. Pass and Dr. Pelech will meet to review any and all procedures and make changes as necessary.*

Figure 9.2.   Protocol sheet for Mrs. Lillie Pass and Dr. James Pelech.

As the figure indicates, the protocol sets goals, identifies tools to achieve those goals, distinguishes the roles of the participants, and establishes an overall evaluation procedure. Obviously, this protocol is a "work in progress." It is not intended to bind the participants. Indeed, even a diplomatic protocol between nations is subject to modification!

9.3.3 Goals and Tasks Worksheet

The Goals and Tasks Worksheet is the "ignition" for the professional development process. It enables all participants to focus on students, create autonomy, create a vision, formulate and analyze goals, and develop and implement an action plan. This worksheet consists of five sections:

- Creating goals and understanding them
- Brainstorming in order to create a goal
- Stating the goal
- Rewording the goal as a question
- Identifying the components for achieving goal

Figure 9.3 shows a completed version of the first four parts of Section I. The figure builds on the protocol sheet and specific example cited earlier. Note that writing was a major activity in this literature class; eventually, writing became a major goal and task.

Goals and Tasks Worksheet

Section I, Parts 1-4: Creating Goals and Understanding These Goals

1. *What are my core values about language arts?*
   o *Understanding a topic at a deeper level*
   o *Translating the understanding of the topic into words*
2. *What student needs should be addressed? What aspects of my personal theories/ core values would I like to change (what personal theories/ core values are being challenged?)? Why?*
   o *Students are not correctly translating their thoughts into words*
   o *Students need to realize that writing is an important part of the understanding literature*
   o *Students not viewing writing as a process, including a monitoring process*
   o *Students are not consistently monitoring the process of changing their thinking*
3. *Why is this bothering me? Why is this so important to me? Would this be as important to other teachers?*
   o *This is a lifelong learning skill which all students should possess*

4. *What do I need to change in order to succeed?*

   o *How to approach the changing of student thinking concerning the writing process*

Figure 9.3.   Prompts I-1 to I-5 of Goals and Tasks Worksheet.

The prompts in Figure 9.3 begin the process of professional development. They not only reactivate core values, they align them with the outcomes of student learning. Looking for discrepancies between core values and student outcomes can begin the process of transforming one's teaching. Identifying the discrepancy between one's values and student outcomes enables an educator to recognize what must be changed, and this represents a foundation of the action plan.

Figure 9.4 displays the remaining prompts for Section I (Parts 5-8) of the worksheet. These can be viewed as continuing the process of developing the action plan by focusing on resources, identifying the helping or hindering forces, and articulating potential benefits and outcomes.

Section I, Parts 5–8: Goals and Tasks Worksheet

What theories or resources could I use? Can I use ideas from other content areas or other topics or other professional development activities? What other teachers can be considered resources?

5.   *Text books, personal resources*

6.   *What are the helping forces?*

   o *Books, personal knowledge, our success with Constructivism, and problem-based learning*

7.   *What are the hindering forces?*

   o *Student resistance to viewing writing as an ongoing process*

8.   *How can this help the rest of the school?*

   o *This (writing as a process) can be a unifying goal or theme for the entire school.*

Figure 9.4.   Prompts I-5 to I-8 of Goals and Tasks Worksheet.

We have pinpointed the discrepancies, what needs to be changed, resources, helping and hindering forces, and possible positive effects for the entire school. Now it is time to create our goals. Section II of the worksheet starts this process by providing suggestions for a brainstorming session (see Figure 9.5). This process enables us to combine the responses from Section I into themes and concepts that then can lead us to a goal statement.

Section II: Goals and Tasks Worksheet

Brainstorming Session—Using Ideas from "I" to Create a Goal and Describe a Goal

- *Students need to value and understand the concept that much knowledge (like writing) is a process, not always getting an answer.*
- *Students must understand how they change their personal thinking.*
- *Students must understand that there are different ways to express one's thoughts, such as writing a poem or acting out a script.*
- *Each way of expressing one's thoughts can change one's thinking.*
- *Monitoring how one express their thoughts, influences how one thinks.*
- *Students must learn and understand that they must change as situations change— they must think differently.*
- *Students must understand that once they change, they must not forget how they have changed and why they have changed.*
- *Monitoring how one thinks and changes actually influences their thinking.*

Figure 9.5.   Brainstorming.

This brainstorming was followed by a synthesis of the ideas. Some of the generalized themes that came out of the synthesis were that knowledge/writing is a process, writing is a part of literature, monitoring how one learns is important, and the process of monitoring is actually a change agent. This synthesis resulted in the statement of the goal, which is Section III of the worksheet and is shown in Figure 9.6.

Section III: Goals and Tasks Worksheet

Goal: Have students understand that writing is an ongoing process and that monitoring changes in this area influences their thinking.

Figure 9.6.   Goal.

Once we have created our goal, we must transform it into a question. While this may seem like a trite point, it is a key point. Let us remember that one of the foundations of our self-inquiry system is asking questions. As pointed out in Chapter 3, questioning not only empowers us to take action, it also is the starting point for creativity. Figure 9.7 displays our goal as a question.

Section IV: Goals and Task Worksheet

How can we as teachers enable students to understand that the writing process is an ongoing process and that monitoring changes in this area influences their thinking?

Figure 9.7.   Restating our goal as a question.

The final section of the worksheet consists of breaking the goal into its components parts and grouping and sequencing these parts into a cohesive system. Figure 9.8 displays the graphic.

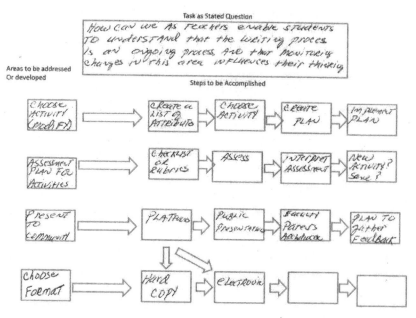

Figure 9.8.   Graphic organizer.

9.3.4 Assessment Plan—Outcomes and Evidence

The assessment plan consists of four parts. The first two parts focus on what you as an educator have learned. The third and fourth parts focus on the students. The examples presented here are from a class Lillie Pass and I were teaching about "tall tales." Tall tales are humorously exaggerated stories of improbable feats.

The assessment begins with prompts concerning our feelings about how well the instruction went (Figure 9.9).

PROMPTS:

- *How did the Tall Tales activity align with my core values?*
- *Did any core values get contradicted?*
- *Did any core values emerge from Tall Tales?*
- *How do I view teaching differently (since Tall Tales)*
- *What new learning theories or techniques emerged? How did this occur?*

Figure 9.9.   Prompts for journal.

If you taught the class alone, you will have to consider these prompts yourself. But if you have team-taught the class, these prompts provide an opportunity for an "interactive" journal, as was introduced in Chapter 6. Let us look here at just one such interactive journal entry (Figure 9.10) from our "tall tales" project and see how it can add to our professional development.

Lillie's entry:

inspiring to watch how some students discussed the different topics that they have.

Jim's response:

It is the word "inspiring" which I want to discuss. [It] implies that there is a higher level of positive emotion or a feeling that stimulates a creative action. Let's dig deeper and see why you felt this way—what is happening that creates this feeling. Also, how does this align with our goal?

Figure 9.10.   Interactive journal entries.

As the response about the single word "inspiring" demonstrates, one aspect of professional development is having the participants connect their activities to their core values or use that knowledge to create new or modify their existing core values. The suggestion of looking further at how the activity was "inspiring" motivates both Lillie and me to evaluate how (or whether) the "tall tales" exercise aligns with our core values.

The next component of the assessment plan comprises prompts for the students (our so-called toll booth passes). Figure 9.11 provides these prompts.

- *What did you learn about the process of writing?*
- *What do you still want to learn about the process of writing?*
- *How did the feedback change your thinking?*
- *What did you learn about writing or teamwork from other group members?*

Figure 9.11.   Prompts for toll booth passes.

The next component of the assessment plan is a short survey given to the students. It provides the opportunity to determine whether student perspectives align with those of the teacher. Figure 9.12 shows an example of the survey administered by Lillie and me.

A. This activity enabled me to understand that writing is a process

Strongly
disagree

Strongly agree

Comments:

B. Monitoring changes to my writing changed the way in which I thought about my
writing

Strongly
disagree

Strongly agree

Figure 9.12.   Student surveys.

Of course, the students' answers to this survey must be taken with a bit of skepticism! Students, even in anonymous surveys, may tend to answer what they believe the teacher wants to hear (or the opposite!). Thus, writing exercises, including worksheets and book exercises, would be an excellent complement.

9.3.5 Project Rubric

The project rubric is designed not solely for making judgments and evaluations but also for guiding the process, including what to do next. The rubric for the process we have been examining in shown in Figure 9.13. Note that at the top of the rubric is the now-familiar goal. The reason for repeating this goal is simple. We need to continuously monitor to make sure that the criteria are connecting with and are leading to the accomplishment of the task.

9.3.6 Action Plan

Though last on our list, the action plan can be used any time during the professional development cycle. An example of an action plan is shown in Figure 9.14. The second column, "Evidence of Completion," is

Goal: How can we as teachers enable students to understand that the writing process is an ongoing process and that monitoring changes in this area influences their thinking?

Criterion/ Component	Still a Vision	In Progress	Completed or Procedures Fully in Place
LEARNING ACTIVITIES TO ACCOMPLISH GOAL			
Create a list of criteria for choosing an activity			
Choose an activity, and create a rationale for this choice			
Create a plan for implementing the activity			
ASSESSMENT PLAN			
Create a list of outcomes or evidence			
Create and choose assessment instruments			
Create checklist for activities			
Interpret the checklist			
Create an action plan			
PRESENTING FINAL PRODUCT			
Platforms decided on: Hard copy Electronic			
Public presentations Principal Parents Archdiocese			
Plan for feedback			

Figure 9.13.   Project rubric.

critical: it must contain concrete evidence that answers the question, "What will I see, hear, touch, or experience?"

9.4 Attending a Conference

Let's talk about what one can do and should do when attending a conference. Some definite actions can be implemented that will lead to transforming one's teaching. Here is a list of ideas that can be helpful.

SAINT ETHELREDA SCHOOL
AND BENEDICTINE UNIVERSITY PARTNERSHIP

2011–2012, MRS. PASS AND DR. PELECH

Goal: How can we as teachers enable students to understand that the writing process is an ongoing process and that monitoring changes in this area influences their thinking?

ACTION	EVIDENCE OF COMPLETION	DATE	COMMENTS/PENDING PLANS

Figure 9.14. Action template.

- Find out whether there are any preconference activities you can join.

- Reflect on what emerging questions are important to your practice.

- Determine what sessions would be beneficial to answering those questions.

- Ask your colleagues whether they know any presenters who may be helpful.

- If possible, make an appointment to meet with these people.

- Since some people may want to learn from you, bring business cards and be ready to discuss your latest work and interests.

- Create a plan for turning the information into action—remember, our vision of knowledge requires a plan for doing this.

A tool that will help is the Conference Planning Sheet. A partially filled-out example is shown in Figure 9.15.

A complementary tool, the New Idea Worksheet, is shown in Figure 9.16. As an illustration, I've filled out the worksheet (in italics) indicating new ideas I learned at a conference and linking them to my core values, an action plan, and an assessment plan.

New Idea Worksheet

Emerging Question	Source of Emerging Question	Importance of Question: Core Value of Teaching? Critical?	Session/Date/ Time/Room	How the Session Will Address the Question
1. Are there more parameters for developing a co-teaching model?	1. Personal experience from working at Saint Ethelreda.	1. Is there a better way of working with Saint E. teachers? Have we developed a model of co-teaching that is research-based?		1. The session will provide research that validates what we already do.
2. Are there instruments for assessing such models?	2. Discussions with Saint E staff	2. How do we know if the present method of co-teaching we use is really helping students? Is it hurting them?		2. The session will present research for using other models
3. What are some sources for learning about co-teaching?	3. Journals	3. We want to know how co-teaching or a particular model of co-teaching can help us with what we already do-constructivism and PBL		3. The session will present new ideas for implementing Constructivism and PBL
	4. Previous conferences indicated the emergence of this topic			

Figure 9.15.   Conference preparation sheet.

115

New Theory/Practice/Framework: Coteaching

Different models were presented at the conference, including "I model, you observe" and station work. A "must" element that must be embedded into any model is that of assessing the model. There must be assessment tools ready to go.

Why it is important? How does it align with my core values? How does it enhance my teaching/my self-inquiry plan/student learning?

The research shows the value of using two teachers in a classroom. Two teachers provide opportunities for station work that can be a source of differentiation (different learning styles, different modes), and this aligns with our Constructivist philosophy and our core values. Another tool for implementing Constructivism is that of the integrated curriculum, and this can be efficiently implemented through coteaching (Ex: one math teacher, one science teacher in the same classroom).

Implementation:

Do own research; (2) Use notes from conference; (3) Discuss with colleagues; (4) Discuss with St. E; (5) Create a plan for implementing at Saint E-include timelines and assessment plan; (6) Find out who the "experts" are; (7) Create a timeline; (8) Insert this into my yearly improvement plan; this fixes accountability for implementing this plan squarely on my shoulders.

Assessment:

Develop formal plan: may include personal journals; observation; student scores, student surveys, video of classes. This assessment may be informal, but may be able to become more formal by formally assigning values to each component.

What other people can I discuss this with? Who else will be interested in this idea?

The "experts," educators who have already implemented coteaching, Saint E. staff and administration

Figure 9.16.   New idea worksheet.

These two worksheets play a key role in professional development. They encourage you to take an active role in a conference—even if you are not "participating" by delivering a presentation or joining in a panel discussion. Not all conferences or workshops are going to transform your teaching; but by asking the right questions ahead of time, you can prepare yourself to get the most out of the meeting. And by evaluating, in writing, what you have learned and how you might apply it, you are more likely to put new ideas into action (and not into the back of your mind!).

9.5 Summary

We have examined another platform for teacher self-inquiry, and that platform is professional development. This chapter has presented ideas and instruments for managing your transformation as a teacher through professional development. These includes examining your goals, building key relationships, and evaluating student outcomes—remembering that the bottom line is that this all goes to improving student learning.

CHAPTER 10

ROLE OF PRESENTER

One role that an educator may assume is that of presenter. This is a visible and well-known role, but it is one that is often misunderstood. In fact, the word "presenter" is a word I considered not using; this word implies that the staff developer is transmitting information to the participants. The system presented throughout this book is, on the contrary, based on the premise that knowledge is constructed, not transmitted. Therefore, we need to realize that in this case "presenter" really means "Constructivist teacher": as a professional-development presenter, your role is more of facilitating the learning process, just as you would be facilitating learning in your classroom.

Not only must you realize that you are enabling other educators to construct their personal transformation, but you also must be cognizant of their special learning needs. Let us review these important concepts.

10.1 Quick Review of Important Concepts

In developing our system of self-inquiry we examined principles of Constructivism. Figure 10.1 summarizes these principles. Note that in our present context, the word "students" refers to teachers who are in the role of students.

Learning Principle 1: Students learn by participating in activities that enable them to create their own version of knowledge. This includes creating rules, definitions, and experiments.

Guide to Transforming Teaching Through Self-Inquiry, pp. 119–128
Copyright © 2013 by Information Age Publishing

Learning Principle 2: Students learn when they teach others, explain to others, or demonstrate a concept to others.

Learning Principle 3: Students learn when they create products from the real world that involve narratives, explanations, justifications, and dialogue.

Learning Principle 4: Knowledge comes in multiple forms, and its development is not uniform; hence, students must be given the opportunity to develop each intelligence or domain.

Learning Principle 5: Students learn when class activities stimulate multiple senses.

Learning Principle 6: Students learn by creating knowledge at different levels of complexity and thinking.

Learning Principle 7: Students learn by connecting new experiences with existing knowledge or connecting previously discrete experiences to each other.

Learning Principle 8: Students learn when they are continuously presented with problems, questions, or situations that force them to think differently.

Learning Principle 9: Students learn by making connections through the "Standard Six": compare and contrast, hypothesize and predict, express understanding in multiple modes, find patterns, summarize, and find personal relevance.

Learning Principle 10: Students regulate their learning by (1) knowing their own ability and learning style preference, (2) analyzing tasks and appropriate strategies, (3) choosing and analyzing appropriate goals, (4) analyzing and appraising their individual level of performance, and (5) managing their time effectively.

Learning Principle 11: Students learn by working with other people who are the source of contradiction, different perspectives, and confirmation.

Learning Principle 12: Modern society provides the source of authentic products for students to produce.

Figure 10.1.   Principles of Constructivism.

We also grouped these principles into four metaphors for teaching; see Figure 10.2.

We know from our previous discussions that the adult learner has some unique characteristics, interests, and needs:

- The adult is a self-directed learner.
- The adult learner constructs knowledge through experience.

Captain of your Ship   TV Reality Show   Turn the Kaleidoscope   Rattle Your Cage
(Autonomy)   (Knowledge is   (Create connections)   (Challenge
                              created in context)   present thinking)

Figure 10.2. Teaching metaphors.

- Readiness, for adult learners, depends on their evolving work and social roles.
- The adult takes a problem-solving orientation to learning.

A few more concepts also deserve mention here. One is developing relationships with participants. As effective teachers we already know that developing a relationship with our students is a key factor for creating an effective student-centered environment. Rogers (1969) tells us that we must establish trust, value their ideas, and make them feel important. Cohen (1990) supports the idea of making participants feel important, while Conant and Norgaard (2011) echoes Rogers' call for developing trust. We all know the importance of looking people in the eye and smiling and how these aid us in developing trust; as Boothman (2010) tells us, making eye contact "engenders trust" and "smiling makes you appear happy and confident" (p. 36).

Arguably, a "one-shot" professional development presentation makes it difficult to develop relationships; but there are actions we can take to start the process.

Fletcher (1983) reminds us that TV commercial and many ads begin with a glimpse of an attractive girl, the reason being that these ads want to get our attention. Now, I am not suggesting that you bring a pretty girl to every one of your presentations, but I really do wish to emphasize the importance of getting participants' attention. According to Fletcher, "to get your audience's attention should be the first and total purpose of the opening words of your speech" (p. 72). Let me repeat: Fletcher recommends that we first get our audience's attention and then follow with a brief introduction. He presents some ideas for this approach, including presenting a startling fact, telling a joke, and complimenting the audience.

Another important technique is providing handouts. Detz (2000) states that "speakers who provide lots of good handouts typically get higher ratings" (p. 55). A note of caution here, however: if participants get the handouts beforehand, they may be paying attention to the handout as opposed to focusing on your words. Detz recommends that you inform the audience that you will pass out the handouts later.

10.2 Guidelines for Facilitating a Presentation

Now, let's put all of our discussion points together to create some guidelines for facilitating a breakout session.

1. Start your presentation *before* the presentation.
   This means that you can build relationships before the official start of your breakout session. Let's look at some possible ideas.

   (a) When you go to other presentations, be sure to meet other people. Talking with others can build a beginning level of trust and an initial interest in other topics and presentations, including your session.

   (b) Use other presentations to generate ideas for your session. While you will be prepared for your session, you can create connections to other presentations, making your session that much better. Additionally, for people who attend this other session along with yours, the connection between the two may go a long way to creating credibility and trust.

   (c) As people enter the room, hand out a small index card for them to fill out. A prototype of this card is shown in Figure 10.3. This card provides information that can make the presentation more meaningful for people. Arguably, if you have fifty people attending your presentation, it will be impossible to go over all of the cards. However, as you work the crowd beforehand (to be discussed in the next paragraph), you can refer to a person's card as you talk with that person. Additionally, you can review the cards after your presentation. You can contact the people whose questions you did not address directly, and you can use their responses to plan for future presentations. It can be used in conjunction with the following activity.

2. Be sure to "work the crowd." We have all witnessed politicians, leaders, and presenters talking to people before or after an event. They seem to make contact with everyone and to know what matters to their audience. By doing so you too can build some initial trust and start the process of building a professional relationship.

> # Name:
> # Email:
> # What you would like to know from this
> # presentation:

Figure 10.3.   Prototype information card.

3. Apply Constructivist principles.

Our system is based on the fact that teacher transformation is a personal construction. So if we are not simply transmitting our own knowledge, how can we help others in their own self-inquiry? Simply put, we need to apply our Constructivist principles to the session. Following are some reminders:

(a) Enable participants to become autonomous.

(b) Enable participants to independently and collaboratively create cognitive connections through comparing/contrasting, creating theories, creating explanations, expressing thoughts in different modes, creating summaries of their learning, and creating personal theories.

(c) Enable participants to create meaningful products and apply newly formed theories in order to improve teaching and/or solve a current classroom problem.

4. Set the conditions for continuing the professional development cycle.

One of our foundations states that we must take our newly learned information and ideas and turn them into action. In the case of a presentation, we must enable the participants to apply their knowledge by translating it into new practices. Let's look at a few ideas that will certainly start and contribute to this process.

(a) As part of the session, be sure that participants create an application of how they plan to apply their knowledge. Also, participants should share their knowledge with participants.

(b) Using the contact information from the index card, contact participants to ensure that they are applying their new knowledge. In doing so, be sure to directly encourage them to create new teaching activities in order to transform teaching.

(c) Using information from the index card, look at questions which you were not able to address. Contact these people with the intention of encouraging them to apply their new knowledge.

(d) Be sure that participants have your contact information before they leave. One way is to staple your business card to your handout sheet.

The following example is taken from a presentation I have made, in which I help teachers translate the Twelve Principles of Constructivism into concrete teaching and learning activities. While it would be convenient simply to give the audience a handout listing these principles (and our four teaching strategies), doing so would defeat the purpose of our system. Instead, I try to prepare handouts that will lead the audience into their own transformation.

In the example presented here, I applied the guidelines from #1. Let's scrutinize certain parts of the handout that drove the session. Figure 10.4 contains Sections A and B. The purpose of Section A is to model how to combine and blend principles together to create a metaphor for teaching using Constructivist principles. It also provides examples of using the newly created metaphoric strategy. I presented a prompt: autonomy (Constructivist teachers believe that learners are autonomous). This teaching strategy came from Principles 1, 2, and 10. I then explained to the participants that the unifying theme of these four principles was that of autonomy, with the metaphor of "Captain of Your Own Ship." We discussed the behaviors that are shown in the diagram and considered how these behaviors could be used in a lesson. Section B presented attendees the opportunity to do this on their own. They were given a prompt: Constructivist teachers believe that people learn in context, using authentic situations and authentic (real-world) thinking skills in order to create authentic products. The participants then were asked to blend principles that align with that prompt and to develop the metaphor and create activ-

Prompt A:

Transforming the Learning Principles Into Teaching Strategies
Autonomy-Constructivist teachers believe that learners are autonomous. This teaching strategy came from Principles 1, 2, and 10.

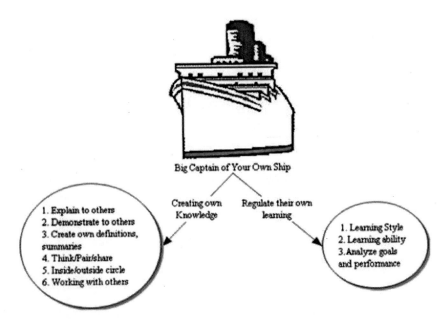

Big Captain of Your Own Ship

Constructivist teachers believe that people learn in context, using authentic situations and authentic (real-world) thinking skills in order to create authentic products.

Prompt B:

What learning principles should we use? Write them in the space provided. What metaphor would you use?

Figure 10.4.   Prompts A and B from handout.

ities for that metaphor. Such an activity follows our guidelines; people must become autonomous, they hypothesize, and they create their own personal theories. In this case I was looking for the blending of Principles 3, 4, and 12 with the metaphor of creating a TV Reality show. Many people came up with other ideas, however, and these ideas led to some rich discussion.

Subsequent activities and sections led to the development of the last two metaphors. As before, attendees developed metaphors that were different from mine but nonetheless resulted in a great learning experience.

After creating new knowledge, it was time for the audience to experience a lesson that was driven by the four metaphors. This next activity (Figure 10.5) is of the utmost importance because it is an example of translating knowledge into action. Participants were asked to experience a lesson structured by the four metaphors. Specifically, in the section of the handout titled "Minilesson," participants were to participate in a lesson about what an effective teacher is. In this lesson people were engaged in Constructivist activities such as analyzing and solving an authentic lesson, creating categories, ranking ideas, applying new ideas, and learning from other groups. Figure 10.5 follows.

Minilesson—Engaging Participants

Let's briefly look at how I would use these principles to teach a lesson from an Education class; the goal of this lesson is to have students examine the characteristics of effective teacher.

You are on a school committee that is assisting the principal in designing a pool of interview questions for perspective teachers. To start this process, she wants you to come up with a list of teacher behaviors (qualities) that represent an effective teacher; then for each behavior (quality) you are to create at least one interview question.

Later she comes and tells you that she may want to show the School Board what her "team" did, so be prepared to create a PowerPoint presentation on what you did and why.

1. *Think/Pair Share: Quietly (by yourself) think of the most effective teacher(s) you have ever had. Write down two (or qualities) that the teacher did that made him (her) effective. Do this is in the space provided.*
2. *Work with your partner to discuss what two behaviors are the most important. Put these two behaviors on the index card provided.*
3. *Get in groups of three to four. Look at everyone's cards in your group, and come up with a top two.*
4. *Board share.*
5. *Categorize/summarize what is put up on the board.*
6. *At your seats (with a partner), write one or two questions for each of the teacher behaviors (qualities) identified.*
7. *I/Spy (Note: this is an activity in which one member of each group goes to other groups in order to obtain other ideas. This member then goes back to his group and reports. Many anecdotal comments indicated that this activity resulted in people changing their metaphors and groupings of principles).*

Figure 10.5.　Minilesson.

While participants by now had experienced a lesson structured by our principles, we know that in order to create a true understanding we must make connections or reflect upon the lesson. Thus, the participants had to reflect on the lesson by making connections and creating new personal theories. The main activities of the lesson were reproduced, and groups of participants met to analyze the components of the minilesson and tell what metaphor it aligned with. The directions for this activity and guidance are shown in Figure 10.6. An important phenomenon occurred during the discussion: many groups decided to alter or change their metaphors or create new ones.

Activity—Analyzing the Minilesson

Directions: For each of the components listed below, you are to align each one with one of your metaphors. Be prepared to discuss your ideas, and do not hesitate to align the activity with more than one metaphor. Additionally, be prepared to discuss any new metaphors

- *Scenario*
- *Think/Pair Share*
- *Work with your partner to discuss what two behaviors are the most important*
- *Get in groups of two to three. Look at everyone's cards in your group, and come up with a top two.*
- *Board share. Categorize/summarize what is put up on the board.*
- *Write one or two questions for each of the behaviors (qualities) identified.*
- *I/Spy*
- *Other activities you feel were important*

Figure 10.6.   Analyzing the lesson.

The final component of the session involved translating this new knowledge into action. Participants were asked to work in a team to create or outline a lesson using the four metaphors or the metaphors that they had created (Figure 10.7). This activity flowed directly from the previous one; participants were now enabled to create a product that was the result of connecting and realigning their concepts from their previous knowledge.

Final Activity—Creating a Lesson

You and your partner(s) are to decide on a lesson you would like to teach by using your knowledge of Constructivism. You are to outline this lesson using your metaphors (the ones I have presented or ones you have created). Be prepared to discuss how the lesson activities align with our principles and your chosen metaphors.

Figure 10.7.   Final activity: Translating knowledge into action.

10.4 The Constructivist Presenter

The role of presenter, as illustrated in this chapter, is clearly more of a facilitator, or motivator. As presenter, I do not assume that I can, or should, tell you how to conduct a class. But I can help you use Constructivist principles to examine your teaching and conference presentations and, as you see the need and the benefits, begin to transform your teaching.

As a presenter at a conference or at a professional development conference, you must remind yourself that the participants are there to learn and that you are there to facilitate their learning. Through the principles presented in this book you can create an environment in which adult self-directed learners can apply ideas from your presentation to accomplish their teaching goals or use your presentation to create applicable practices to their teaching.

CHAPTER 11

PROFESSIONAL PORTFOLIOS

How many times have we heard the question "What's your evidence?" or the demand "Show me the facts"? These serve as the rationale for teaching portfolios. A teaching portfolio is the platform for providing concrete and visible evidence of one's skills, knowledge, identity, and growth as a teacher.

11.1 Portfolios as Platforms for Transformation

A teaching portfolio certainly fits into our system of self-inquiry and transformation. In discussing student portfolios Johnson, Mims-Cos, and Doyle-Nichols (2010) state that a portfolio can enable "a student to engage in higher levels of thinking through the use of inquiry and reflection" (p.5). This idea can be applied to portfolios developed by teachers. Can reflections in portfolios lead to transformation? Tigelaar, Dolmans, De Grave, Wolfhagen, and van der Vleuten (2006) provide us some ideas on this. In discussing the reflection frameworks for medical school teachers they encourage the increased use of frameworks that address beliefs, identity, and mission. These are parameters that can drive transformation. To transform one's teaching, one must change the nature of one's identity as a teacher, and this involves examining one's beliefs and mission as a teacher. The professional portfolio provides this opportunity by empowering the teacher to identify artifacts and to reflect on these. How does one create a professional portfolio? What does one put into a professional portfolio? How can our four metaphors be used to guide the development of a professional portfolio? Below are some prompts, associated with our now-familiar four metaphors, that can aid us in developing a portfolio, not only by documenting our transformation, but also by enabling that transformation.

Captain of Your Own Ship

- What are my core values?
- What is my identity as a teacher?
- Have my meaning schemes and core values changed?
- What artifacts from my daily teaching represent my core values and identity?

TV Reality Show

- What themes currently guide my teaching?
- Does my school or university have prescribed parameters for guiding the creation of the portfolio?
- What school initiatives or guidelines are required for me to implement?
- What artifacts provide evidence for my use of school initiatives or guidelines?
- What procedures are not working?
- What procedures are most important?
- What latitude do I have for change?
- Do I have the resources for change?
- Am I doing something that does not align with my core values? Do I have artifacts to back this up?

Turn the Kaleidoscope

- Is my role as a teacher changing? Why?
- Am I developing new personal theories? Why?
- Do I need to develop new personal theory?
- What artifacts of my teaching have meaning for me?
- Do my present teaching artifacts indicate that it is time for a change?
- What patterns or themes are seen through class artifacts?

- How do emerging patterns or themes align with my personal theories?
- Do emerging patterns or themes require the construction of a new perspective?
- What are the helping or hindering forces for creating new goals or perspectives?
- How can I blend new knowledge bases with present core values in order to create new personal theories or to transform my teaching? What kind of artifacts would show this?
- How will I use new theories or artifacts in the future?
- What is my action plan?

Rattling Your Cage

- What is bothering me? Why?
- What if I altered or changed one of my present artifacts? Would it still align with my core values and underlying assumptions?
- What would I have to change in an artifact in order to challenge personal theories?
- How would a different assumption or different teaching theory change my present artifacts?
- What surprised me?
- Do my present artifacts represent my assumptions concerning power and equity?
- How can I use an artifact so it transforms teaching in a manner different from its original use?

11.2 Tools for the Portfolio

What are the instruments that put these prompts into motion? The tools described in the following sections were developed for use in an electronic environment. Using an electronic environment has several advantages. One obvious advantage is that it saves paper. Another advantage is ease of navigation. Figure 11.1 shows the slide I used to illustrate the three guiding parameters or sections in my own portfolio. By clicking on any one of the three, one can go directly to that area of the portfolio. The three main sections of the portfolio align with the prompts "What themes or parameters guide my teaching?" and "What school initiatives or guidelines are required for me to implement?" The four sections of the logo represent the four hallmarks of the School of Education, and the logo is connected to the three parameters guiding the portfolio.

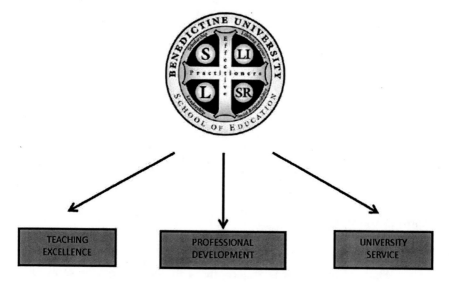

Figure 11.1.   Guiding parameters of sample teacher's portfolio.

Let's look at the components of the portfolio.

1. Prologue—this document contains an introduction and acknowledgments
2. Conceptual Framework of the Portfolio
3. Overviews of Main Sections
4. Artifacts and Rationale
5. Action Plan and Action Matrix
6. Philosophy of Learning
7. Curriculum Vitae
8. Letters of Support

We will now examine the components 2–5.

11.3 Portfolio Conceptual Framework

The Conceptual Framework provides an overview of the portfolio. Through a narrative and a graphical organizer/logo this document describes the teaching identity of the educator. Figure 11.2 shows the graphical organizer/logo.

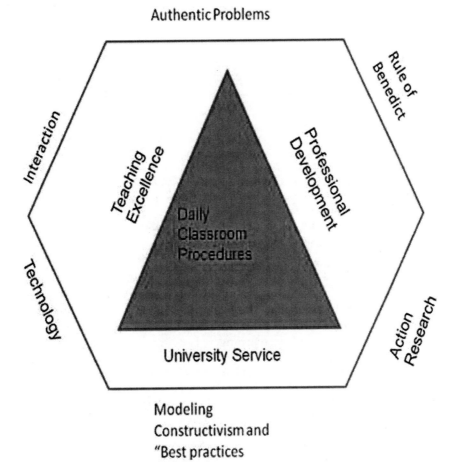

Authentic Problems

Rule of Benedict

Interaction

Teaching Excellence

Professional Development

Daily Classroom Procedures

Technology

University Service

Action Research

Modeling
Constructivism and
"Best practices

Figure 11.2.   Sample of graphical organizer/logo for portfolio.

Figure 11.2 provides at a glance insight into the basic foundations of my portfolio. Three parameters set down by the university (Teaching Excellence, Professional Development, and University Service) form the sides of the triangle: they represent my everyday teaching. (I will not discuss University Service except to note that some of the committees on which I served, including the Core Committee and 2+2 Task Force, did influence my teaching.) The six sides of the hexagon form the components of my teaching identity and align with the follow prompts:

- What is my identity as a teacher?
- What themes currently guide my teaching?

- Does my school or university have prescribed parameters for guiding the creation of the portfolio?

The narrative describes the development of the professional identity of the educator. Let's look at some excerpts of my own narrative. The first excerpt (Fig. 11.3) discusses the component of Constructivism so important to my development.

> *It became obvious to me that people create their own knowledge, as compared to having knowledge transferred to them. This was the beginning of my alignment with the Constructivist philosophy of learning. Very briefly, the Constructivist philosophy believes that knowledge is a subjectively created entity that is constructed in an environment of inquiry, investigation, and invention with the processes of problem-solving, cognitive conflict, and reflection playing major roles. I did not know that I was a Constructivist at the time, but in terms of spirit and intent, I was fast becoming a believer in the Constructivist philosophy.*

Figure 11.3.   Example of narrative for introduction to portfolio.

The next excerpt discusses a more advanced stage in my development as an educator. In particular, the example (Fig. 11.4) shows how using authentic problems through problem-based learning (PBL) emerged as a defining characteristic of my teaching.

> *My studies for the CAS were interrupted in early 1996. As a Lieutenant Colonel in the Army Reserves, I was activated for Operation Joint Endeavor. As a staff officer for a command that controlled all logistical operations in Europe and Africa, one of my functions was to coordinate with civilian (European and American) transportation companies. This experience enabled me to think about how successful people survive in the "real world." Admittedly, I was somewhat mortified by my conclusions. Not once did I solve a quadratic equation, nor did I have to determine the domain of a trigonometric function. What was essential for survival in the business world? It was a mental disposition and framework for solving messy and ill-defined problems that may have more than one solution (as opposed to traditional word problems in school). I returned to civilian life and my CAS studies with the mindset of blending this experience with my Constructivist philosophy and my desire to include authentic problems (applications) into my teaching.*

> *After finishing my CAS, I enrolled in the Doctorate Program in Curriculum and Instruction at National Louis University (while still teaching at Richards High School.) It was during my doctoral studies that I came upon the platform of Problem-Based Learning (PBL). PBL aligned nicely with my goal of embedding authentic problems into my Constructivist philosophy. In fact, PBL is one of the instruments that I now use to implement the Constructivist philosophy. It is during the final years at Richards that I formally used the PBL platform.*

Figure 11.4.   Excerpt from narrative component of portfolio.

11.4 Overview of Main Sections

While the Introductory Letter and Conceptual Framework provide background information and a broad perspective of the entire portfolio, the Overview for each section focuses on how each section and each artifact (to be discussed in the next section) contribute to the transformation process. Figure 11.5 contains an excerpt from the Overview of the professional development section of my portfolio. The excerpt examines how my role as a teacher has changed from the local level, my classroom and university, to a larger venue, that being national and international audiences. These "new" audiences signify that I have been growing toward more leadership responsibilities. This excerpt from the Overview is driven by the following prompts:

- Is my role as a teacher changing?
- Have my meaning schemes changed?

The area of Professional Development not only enhances my teaching persona, it extends this persona into a new dimension, and this element is Leader and Professional Developer. By publishing and presenting at conferences and hosting conferences, I have been able to expand my venue from the local Benedictine community to a national and international platform. Administering and participating in grants provided another platform for growing as a leader and professional developer. These venues have provided the opportunity to be a leader in varying areas of education, and this represents my growth from a classroom teacher to a multifaceted educator.

The artifact "The Comprehensive Handbook for Constructivist Teaching" is my book, which was published by Information Age Publishing in January 2010. It is not only the formalization of my Constructivist principles; it is another step toward being a leader in the Constructivist movement. The artifact for this book also contains a copy of a part of a web site of an educator from Poland who purchased my book and asked permission to reprint my principles of Constructivism, which are in the book on his web site (English and Polish). This has expanded my leadership to the international level.

Figure 11.5.   Excerpt from Overview of professional development section of portfolio.

11.5 Artifacts, Rationales, and Examples

Artifacts are the tangible evidence that one not only has met professional standards but also has undergone a transformation—has grown—

as an educator. Let us take a look at some artifacts, realizing that the list represents only a small portion of the possibilities.

- Philosophy of learning
- Sample lesson plans
- Quizzes
- Tests
- Rubrics
- Student work
- Video clips of one's teaching
- Evaluations
- Action research projects
- Audio clips of interviews from action research projects
- Curriculum maps
- Curriculum guides
- Documents from summer academic camps
- Student testimonials
- Committee reports
- Published review of articles and books
- Published articles
- Published books
- Documentation of professional development work
- Documentation of conference presentations
- Documentation of hosting conferences
- Documentation of grants
- Documentation of speaking engagements
- Documentation of working on scholarship committees
- Documentation of task force work
- Documentation of work with student honor societies

Artifacts by themselves do not provide evidence for one's transformation. I cannot prove that I played college baseball by bringing in a bat; I must provide concrete evidence such as box scores, official rosters, team pictures, or official letters from the coaching staff. The same is true for portfolios. Accompanying each artifact, therefore, is a rationale, or set of reasons, for why the artifact is important in one's transformation. Figure 11.6 shows the template I used in my portfolio for this purpose.

Title of artifact:

What the artifact is:

Why the artifact is important:

What I learned:

What I will do in the future:

Figure 11.6.   Template for artifact analysis.

The examples in the rest of this chapter will illustrate how the prompts help me articulate the transformation of my own teaching. I begin in Figure 11.7 with an analysis of an artifact that contains the program and personal planning notes from a conference for which I not only gave a presentation but also worked as a facilitator for professional development. This artifact is evidence of two of my teacher identity components, modeling and authentic situations; it is also evidence of the expansion of my role into professional development.

Title of artifact: _Presenting at the Institute for Learning Centered Education Constructivist Conference_

What the artifact is: _This artifact contains documentation of my participation and presentation at this conference in the summers of 2007 and 2008. My participation included delivering professional development (serving as a facilitator/coach) for a group of teachers working on school initiatives._

Why the artifact is important: _At these conferences I continued the process of "expanding" my hallmarks of PBL and delivering Constructivism. I presented my vision of Constructivism to an audience that ranged beyond Benedictine University. I presented on PBL and the Bridging Question Strategy (BQS), which became a series of articles for the Journal for the Practical Application of Constructivism in Education._

My role as an educator is now expanding past my role as a classroom teacher. I must now consider my role as someone who coaches other teachers. My audience has now grown geographically and now includes other professionals. A new role such as delivering professional development provides an opportunity for developing personal theories concerning working with other teachers.

What I learned: _I learned that there is a nationwide initiative by practicing teachers to translate the Constructivist philosophy into concrete, observable behaviors. This is_ *especially so in mathematics education. I discovered that many practitioners, while interested in PBL as an instructional delivery system, do not understand the "nuts and bolts" of the process; also, many educators, while believing that PBL is a form of Constructivism, are not able to articulate this alignment. This brings up a very important point. Like any content one must not only learn it, but also learn it well enough to present or teach it so people will learn. I am now turning my attention to teaching about Constructivism and PBL.*

I learned that while I have many personal theories about student learning and motivation, I must develop theories concerning the learning and motivation of adult learners. Their motivation and learning styles differ from those of traditional-aged students.

<u>*What I will do in the future:*</u> *A very important initiative to pursue is that of learning about the adult learner. The adult learner learns differently from the traditional-aged student, and this mandates conducting research on the adult learner. I plan to create guidelines concerning the adult learner and use these to guide future professional development work. A parallel goal is that of developing lesson plans on the teaching of Constructivism and PBL.*

Figure 11.7.   Artifact analysis showing expanding role into professional development.

Figures 11.8 and 11.9 illustrate an artifact that not only demonstrates one of the defining parameters of my teaching, authentic problems, but also presents the artifact as a tool for future use in a different capacity—in this case expanding my role to that of teacher educator or professional developer. This artifact and its analysis demonstrate how an artifact can have two purposes. First, it can provide evidence for an aspect of one's teaching; second, it can demonstrate another component of one's teaching or can demonstrate how that artifact may lead to teacher transformation. Figure 11.8 contains the narrative and the diagram that make up the problem. Figure 11.9 contains the rationale document.

The Abstract Art Problematic

You are an art dealer and a very rich art collector has handed this sketch to you and told you that he is looking for the original painting of the figure below. He said that he would give you $2,000.00 if you can get the original for him within the next 2 hours. You think your friend in New York actually has it, but your fax machine is broken, so you decide to call your friend and describe it to him. What directions should you dictate to him?

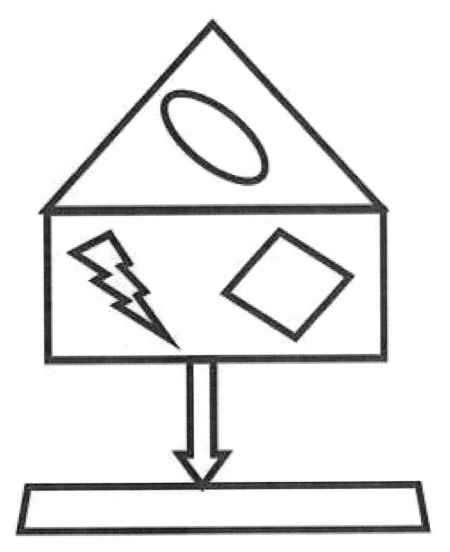

Figure 11.8.   Artifact from abstract art.

<u>*Title of artifact:*</u> *Saint E. Abstract Art Problem*

What the artifact is: *The artifact is the authentic problem given to students. The class was currently on the topic of classifying polygons, and this handout translates that topic into an authentic situation.*

Why the artifact is important: *The topic of classifying polygons can be dry and uninspiring for students, as well as for the teacher. This Problematic addresses this issue by translating polygons into an authentic situation. This will serve as a model for the Saint Ethelreda staff as to how curriculum topics can be used as the basis for authentic situations. Using authentic situations as a driving force of my pedagogy is an important component of my teaching identity, and this artifact presents evidence of this.*

While the problematic was designed to align with polygons, it also presents the concept of angles and rotation. By bringing in a second and possibly third concept this problematic does two important things. First, it demonstrates that authentic problems contain more than one topic, and second, it presents the concept of "spiral learning." Spiral learning is an aspect of Constructivist philosophy that states that students can learn a topic at a one level of learning and spiral back to it later on and relearn it at a higher level. In this case angles and rotations are examined at a surface level, with a formal investigation to occur later.

What I learned: This problematic clearly demonstrated that middle school students do a great deal of their thinking at the concrete operational level. This is a constant reminder that definitions must be presented by starting with the students' concrete-level words and then scaffolding to the abstract generalizations. I also learned that the teacher must be ready to link student concrete learning to the abstract representation.

What I will do in the future: Introducing the practice of "spiral learning" will be included in my methods classes. Where I have created principles of Constructivism for my teaching, these must be reevaluated to specifically present this concept.

I will also continue to use this Problematic in my teaching at Saint Ethelreda. This Problematic has been very effective in helping students learn and understand the different types of polygons.

I plan to use this artifact in a different capacity. The next time I present this lesson, I will tape it so I can use it in my presentations, teacher preparation classes, and in delivering professional development. While this was not the original intent of the artifact, its purpose has now been transformed.

Figure 11.9.   Artifact analysis showing transformation of original purpose.

One component of transforming teaching is analyzing our underlying assumptions; by doing so, the teacher may find that practices meant to be helpful were actually a hindrance (critical reflection). Figure 11.10 shows an analysis of an artifact that consisted of the audio recording I conducted for my action research at Benedictine University. The reflections in the artifact analysis illustrate how the practice of transcribing an interview can have negative effects.

Title of artifact: Interview for Action Research

What the artifact is: Portion of the interview of one of my students that was used in my action Research. It was downloaded from my digital recorder. Written permission from the student for use of her interview is also included.

Why the artifact is important: This artifact is important for several reasons:

1. *It is an example of my use of technology, which solidifies my teacher persona as a user and implementer of technology.*
2. *Since this was a part of my own Action Research, I was modeling for students this tool.*
3. *I modeled for students the use of technology in their own research.*
4. *Interviews are an essential tool for Action Research, so not only was I modeling for students, I provided an opportunity for them to experience this authentic task.*
5. *In conducting this interview, I used the technique of an "ethnographic interview." Briefly, this technique does not ask people what is meaningful or why; rather, it asks people to describe what they would do in the natural setting of the phenomenon. It also asks people to compare and contrast behaviors in their natural setting.*
6. *In conducting and analyzing the interviews, I used the basic four teaching strategies from Chapter 4 of my book (another artifact). These were easily transferred to conducting and interpreting an interview.*

<u>*What I learned:*</u> *I learned the utility of using technology such as the digital recorder. The easy storage and the ability to replay the interview provided great dividends.*

I also learned the power of qualitative data such as interviews. Real meaning can be constructed by the researcher when the actual words of an interviewee are analyzed.

Student responses indicated that by going through the interview themselves they realized how technology (the digital recorder) can be a powerful tool for obtaining qualitative data.

There is a "down" side to using recording interviews, and that is the process of transcribing the tapes. This was a very long and arduous process, and I wonder if the hours it took were really worth it. The hours required to transcribe the interviews resulted in a great deal of frustration, and this negatively influenced my rational interpretation of the interviews.

<u>*What I will do in the future:*</u> *I will continue to use the digital recorder in my own Action Research and will use it as I teach about qualitative data. In fact, I will include in my lesson plan a discussion of how technology influences the data it is meant to collect.*

In terms of technology, I did realize that the manual transcription of tapes is an almost impossible job. I learned that technology should also be used for transcription purposes.

Since my practice is structured by the Constructivist principle of connecting different knowledge bases of different information, it will become very important to emphasize the connecting of quantitative and qualitative data; this will involve the process of creating a framework.

I must also address the issue of what to do with the challenges presented by transcribing the interviews. Since the frustration resulting from the transcription process has a negative effect on my research, such as hindering the rational analysis of the interview, it is an issue that must be addressed.

Figure 11.10.   Analysis showing possible limitations of artifact.

Another example of critical reflection emerges from the next artifact. This is the artifact in which my Secondary Math Methods class worked with the Secondary Science Methods class to create and teach a cross-curricular lesson that blended math and science concepts. Not only does this artifact illustrate critical reflection, it also is an example of an artifact that has more than one component. The first component (not shown) is a document examining the importance of the cross-curricular approach in education, especially education for preservice teachers. The second component (Fig. 11.11) is a portion of the description of the project. The third component (Fig. 11.12) is a copy of the results of the survey students filled out. The fourth component (Fig. 11.13) is a reflection on this artifact.

SECONDARY SCIENCE METHODS AND SECONDARY MATHEMTICS METHODS COLLABORATION PROJECT

In the spirit of collaboration as a professional teaching standard, students from the Secondary Science Methods and Secondary Mathematics Methods classes are teamed together to do a collaborative teaching project. The purpose of this is to promote collaborative relationships and partnerships with colleagues from different content areas.

The collaborative teams

In the fall semester we will have 3 science methods students and 9 math methods students, and they will form 3 collaborative teams, with each team consisting of 1 science methods student, and 3 math methods students.

The assignment

Each collaborative team will prepare and teach a lesson using the School of Education Lesson Plan template to support at least one science content standard and one math content standard. Each team will be given 40 minutes for the teaching assignment during the last weeks of the fall semester (dates to be determined).

Figure 11.11.   Artifact: cross-curricular project, second component.

Preservice Teachers Efficacy* Perception Survey

	Percentage of Agree and Strongly Agree in the Pre-Survey	Percentage of Agree and Strongly Agree in the Post-Survey
I am confident in my ability to:		
1. Create integrated lessons and units	75	100
2. Establish a feeling of learning community in my work (school)	92	92
3. Use different activities and curricula in teaching	100	100
4. Teach content as a coninquirer with my colleagues	33	100
5. Locate resources for preparing an interdisciplinary lesson	75	83
6. Develop lessons to support the Illinois Learning Standards (ILS)	84	92
7. Use cooperative teaching techniques	92	100
8. Use basic concepts in my content area to reinforce the concept in a different area	75	100
9. Implement teaching strategies that incorporate inquiry-based learning	66	92
10. Provide concrete and real world experiences in teaching	83	100
11. Take calculated risks in trying new teaching ideas	72	83

*Efficacy is defined as the ability to produce the intended results. The survey assesses the perception of math and science methods students to support ILTS#9 (Collaborative Relationships) and ILTS#10 (Reflection and Professional Growth).

Figure 11.12.   Artifact: Cross-curricular project, third component.

Title of artifact: Cross–Curricular Project

What the artifact is: This artifact describes a cross-curricular project that my Middle/ High School Math Methods class participated in with Dr. Wong and his Middle/High School Science Methods class. The purpose of this activity was to have students in both classes create and implement a secondary/middle school-level class using the domains of science and math. This artifact has four components. The first component is a document examining the importance of the cross-curricular approach in education, especially education for preservice teachers. The second component is a packet that presents the components of this project. The third component is a copy of the results of the survey students filled out. The fourth component is a reflection on this artifact.

Why the artifact is important: This artifact is important because it demonstrates the ability to make curricular adjustments to help prepare preservice teachers for teaching in the twenty-first century. This Cross-Curricular Project is an example of modeling and implementing the Constructivist philosophy. The hallmark of interaction enters into this artifact; math methods students had to interact and collaborate with science methods students. Student comments indicated that they realized that collaboration is a complex, multidiscipline process that must be studied in order to be implemented effectively.

Another important aspect of this artifact is that it involved interaction between students and instructor. The results of the survey served as an instrument for a rich class discussion.

What I learned doing the artifact: The implementation of cross-curricular teaching is a multifaceted endeavor. This includes different vocabularies and different frame of minds for different content areas.

Another important concept which developed was that effective collaboration is more than something that we do at a particular time in class. It is more of a mindset or a means of relating to people. It is something one must learn to do, and it is something that must be constructed mentally and emotionally by students.

What I will do in the future: In collaboration with Dr. Wong, I will be analyzing the results of the survey, and using this analysis to plan for further collaboration projects such as this. I also plan to work with Dr. Wong on extending this project into both of our Middle/High School methods courses. Also, I will work on developing a framework for structuring the art and science of collaboration. Collaboration must be presented to students as an entity formed by cognitive science and sociological principles.

This artifact must be examined from another perspective, namely, that this endeavor may inadvertently hurt students. While we are spending time on coteaching, we are losing time on how to teach by ourselves, which is what we will do most of the time. Additionally, time spent on learning how to implement the science topic could be used to learn how to teach mathematics topics—and this is the purpose of the class. We may need to focus on the main objective of this course.

Figure 11.13.　Analysis of the cross-curricular project.

11.6 Action Plan and Action Matrix

A quick recall of the foundations of our system of self-inquiry reminds us that we must take our experience and new information and *translate it into action.* Pfeffer and Sutton (2000), when discussing organizations that turn knowledge into action, argue that the change in attitude follows change in behavior: "People will know—learn—from the doing" (p. 65). Thus, we must now use our newly created information and transform it into knowledge by taking action on that information. The tool used is the action plan; indeed, I have such a plan for each major section of my portfolio.

Let's look at some of the parts of my action plan for the section on Teaching Excellence. Figure 11.14 shows the first part. The main body contains four of the components of my teaching identity. (For logistical and administrative reasons, Constructivism was used as the umbrella concept for the Constructivist philosophy, PBL, and authentic problems.) The circles outside the box represent the platforms for analyzing Teaching Excellence. Note that originally there were three components, but through growth and transformation "research" emerged as another platform.

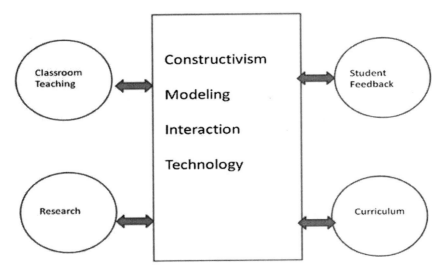

Figure 11.14.   Action plan for Teaching Excellence.

The main body of the action plan must discuss growth areas. Therefore, let us look at an excerpt from the research section, which has emerged as a platform for analyzing my teaching (Figure 11.15).

The final component (though not last in importance) is research. The artifact from the Action Research conducted in my EDUC 310 class has already been discussed in terms of how it will change my teaching. Additionally, the future use of this artifact indicated that action research should be conducted with our partnership elementary school. This research will focus on student perception of the effectiveness of Constructivist activities. The possible research questions are:

From the perspectives of Saint Ethelreda students, what are the outcomes of Constructivist activities conducted in class?

From the perspective of Saint Ethelreda students, how do the outcomes of Constructivist activities compare with the outcomes of traditional teaching?

From the perspectives of Saint Ethelreda students, what is the value of the outcomes of Constructivist activities in comparison to the value of outcomes from traditional teaching?

Additionally, the goal of conducting action research at Saint Ethelreda shows the emerging importance of action research in my teaching. With the emergence of my own action research projects, and the emergence across the teaching profession of "teacher as researcher," it is easy to see that my role in the classroom is taking on a new dimension—that of action researcher.

Figure 11.15.   Excerpt from research component of action plan.

Having documented changes and the plan for future changes, we must now translate these ideas into concrete actions. The instrument for this is the action matrix (Figure 11.16), in which we list the goals, the tangible evidence for requiring action, and what still needs to be done.

Action Matrix

Goals	*Evidence for translating into action*	*Status*
Increase the authenticity of my Problematics by using SKYPE for "real-time" interviews with practitioners who will be the focus of the next Problematic	After action report on the effectiveness of the interview Student reflections from exit passes	Completed
Increase authenticity by videotaping student-led discussions and by using a student-constructed rubric to evaluate the lesson.	Lesson plan on creating rubrics Student-created rubric Completed rubric File of videos	Two more students must give presentations.
Examine the perceptions of middle school students concerning the effectiveness of Constructivist teaching activities	Completed student surveys Completed transcripts of student interviews Completed action plans for next cycle of research	Three more students must be interviewed. Last cycle of action plan must be completed.

Figure 11.16.   Action matrix for action plan.

11.7 Portfolios and Teacher Self-Inquiry

While many people believe that portfolios just *present evidence* of one's growth, they actually do much more than that. With the prompts from our four metaphors to guide the creation of a portfolio, a portfolio can become the tool that *leads to further growth and helps transform* one's teaching. Inquiry can be thought of as the process of collecting, selecting, sorting, analyzing, and evaluating artifacts; and since the four metaphors provide the guiding questions for this process, the portfolio is actually the driving force behind the self-inquiry process.

REFERENCES

Alvermann, D. E. (1981). The compensatory effect of graphic organizers on descriptive text. *Journal of Educational Research, 75*(1), 44-48.

Argyris, C., & Schön, D. A. (1992). *Theory in practice: Increasing professional effectiveness.* San Francisco, CA: Jossey-Bass.

Batt, T., & Wilson, S. (2008). A study of voice-recognition software as a tool for teacher response. *Computers and Composition, 25*(2), 165-181. doi:10.1016/j.compcom.2008.01.004

Ball, D. L., & Cohen, D. K. (1999). Developing practice, developing practitioners: toward a practice-based theory of professional development. In L. Darling-Hammond & G. Skyes (Eds.), *Teaching as the learning professional: Handbook of policy and practice* (pp. 3-32). San Francisco, CA: Jossey-Bass.

Bellanca, J. A. (2009). *Designing professional development for change: A guide for improving classroom instruction* (2nd ed.). Thousand Oaks, CA: Corwin Press.

Belmonte, D. (2003). *Teaching from the deep end: Succeeding with today's classroom challenges.* Thousand Oaks, CA: Corwin Press.

Black, A. L., & Halliwell, G. (2000). Accessing practical knowledge: How? why? *Teaching and Teacher Education, 16*(1), 103-115. doi:10.1016/S0742051X(99)00045-1

Boothman, N. (Ed.). (2010). *Convince them in 90 seconds or less: Make instant connections that pay off in business and in life.* New York, NY: Workman.

Boyer, E. L. (1990). *Scholarship reconsidered: Priorities of the professoriate.* Princeton, NJ: Carnegie Foundation for the Advancement of Teaching.

Brewster, C., & Northwest Regional Educational Laboratory. (2003, December). *Building trust with schools and diverse families: A foundation for lasting partnerships.* Portland, OR: Northwest Regional Educational Laboratory.

Brookfield, S. (1995). *Becoming a critically reflective teacher.* San Francisco, CA: Jossey-Bass.

Bruce, C. D., Esmonde, I., Ross, J., Dookie, L., & Beatty, R. (2010). The effects of sustained classroom-embedded teacher professional learning on teacher efficacy and related student achievement. *Teaching and Teacher Education, 26*(8), 1598-1608. doi:10.1016/j.tate.2010.06.011

Burmark, L. (2002). *Visual literacy: Learn to see, see to learn.* Alexandria, VA.: Association for Supervision and Curriculum Development.

Cell, E. (1984). *Learning to learn from experience*. Albany, NY: State University of New York Press.

Clarke, L. (2009). Video reflections in initial teacher education. *British Journal of Educational Technology, 40*(5), 959-961. doi:10.1111/j.14678535.2008.00896.x

Cohen, W. A. (1990). *The art of the leader*. Englewood Cliffs, NJ: Prentice Hall.

Cole, A. L., & Knowles, J. G. (2000). *Researching teaching: Exploring teacher development through reflexive inquiry*. Boston, MA: Allyn & Bacon.

Collier, S. T. (1999). Characteristics of reflective thought during the student teaching experience. *Journal of Teacher Education, 50*(3), 173-181. doi:10.1177/002248719905000303

Conant, D. R., & Norgaard, M. (2011). *TouchPoints: Creating powerful leadership connections in the smallest of moments*. San Francisco, CA: Jossey-Bass.

Connelly, F. M., & Clandinin, D. J. (1990). Stories of experience and narrative inquiry. *Educational Researcher, 19*(5), 2-14. doi:10.3102/0013189X019005002

Costa, A. L., & Garmston, R. J. (1994). *Cognitive coaching: A foundation for renaissance schools*. Norwood, MA.: Christopher-Gordon.

Costello, P. J. M. (2003). *Action research*. London, England: Continuum.

Dana, N. F., & Yendol-Hoppey, D. (2009). *The reflective educator's guide to classroom research: Learning to teach and teaching to learn through practitioner inquiry* (2nd ed.). Thousand Oaks, CA: Corwin Press.

Darling-Hammond, L., & Richardson, N. (2009). Teacher learning: What matters? *Educational Leadership, 66*(5), 46-53.

Denzin, N. K., & Lincoln, Y. S. (2003). *The landscape of qualitative research: Theories and issues* (2nd ed.). Thousand Oaks, CA: SAGE.

Detz, J. (2007). *It's not what you say, it's how you say it: Ready-to-use advice for presentations, speeches and other speaking occasions, large and small*. New York, NY: Bristol Park Books.

Dobbins, R. (1996). The challenge of developing a "reflective practicum." *Asia-Pacific Journal of Teacher Education, 24*(3), 269-280.

Farrell, T. S. C. (2004). *Reflective practice in action: 80 reflection breaks for busy teachers*. Thousand Oaks, CA: Corwin Press.

Fletcher, L. (1983). *How to speak like a pro*. New York, NY: Ballantine.

Fogarty, R., & Pete, B. M. (2007). *From staff room to classroom: A guide for planning and coaching professional development*. Thousand Oaks, CA: Corwin Press.

Fullan, M. (2008). *The six secrets of change: What the best leaders do to help their organizations survive and thrive*. San Francisco, CA: Jossey-Bass.

Garner, P. (1997). In-service teachers' use of graphical accounts to illuminate aspects of their practice in special educational needs. *Teacher Development, 1*(2), 281-291.

Ghaye, T. (2007). Is reflective practice ethical? (the case of the reflective portfolio). *Reflective Practice, 8*(2), 151-162. doi:10.1080/14623940701288859

Giorgi, A. (1997). The theory, practice, and evaluation of the phenomenological method as a qualitative research. *Journal of Phenomenological Psychology, 28*(2), 235-260.

Goldberg, M. C. (1998). *The art of the question: A guide to short-term question-centered therapy*. New York, NY: Wiley.

Goodlad, J. I. (1994). *Educational renewal: Better teachers, better schools*. San Francisco, CA: Jossey-Bass.

Gudmundsdottir, S. (1990). Values in pedagogical content knowledge. *Journal of Teacher Education, 41*(3), 44-52. doi:10.1177/002248719004100306

Guskey, T. R. (2000). *Evaluating professional development*. Thousand Oaks, CA: Corwin Press.

Guskey, T. R., & Yoon, K. S. (2009). What works in professional development? *Phi Delta Kappan, 90*(7), 495-500.

Harpaz, I., Balik, C., & Ehrenfeld, M. (2004). Concept mapping: An educational strategy for advancing nursing education. *Nursing Forum, 39*(2), 27-30.

Haycock, K. (1998). *Good teaching matters ... a lot*. Santa Cruz, CA: Center for the Future of Teaching & Learning.

Hendricks, C. (2009). *Improving schools through action research: A comprehensive guide for educators* (2nd ed.). Upper Saddle River, NJ: Pearson.

Hobbs, V. (2007). Faking it or hating it: Can reflective practice be forced? *Reflective Practice, 8*(3), 405-417. doi:10.1080/14623940701425063.

Hunt, D. E. (1976). Teachers' adaptation: "Reading" and "flexing" to students. *Journal of Teacher Education, 27*(3), 268-275. doi:10.1177/0022487176027 00323

Interstate New Teacher Assessment and Support Consortium & Council of Chief State School Officers. (2011). *InTASC model core teaching standards a resource for state dialogue*. Retrieved from http://bibpurl.oclc.org/web/42622; http://bibpurl.oclc.org/web/42622;http://www.ccsso.org/Documents/2011InTASC %20Model%20Core%20Teaching%20Standards_April%202011.pdf

Johnson, G. C. (2001). Accounting for pre-service teachers' use of visual metaphors in narratives. *Teacher Development, 5*(1), 119-140.

Johnson, G. C. (2002). Using visual narrative and poststructuralism to (re)read a student teachers's professional practice. *Teaching and Teacher Education, 18*, 387-404.

Johnson, G. C. (2004). Reconceptualising the visual in narrative inquiry into teaching. *Teaching and Teacher Education, 20*(5), 423-434.

Johnson, C. C., & Fargo, J. D. (2010). Urban school reform enabled by transformative professional development: Impact on teacher change and student learning of science. *Urban Education, 45*(1), 4-29. doi:10.1177/ 0042085909352073

Johnson, G. C. (2004). Reconceptualising the visual in narrative inquiry into teaching. *Teaching and Teacher Education, 20*(5), 423-434. doi:10.1016/ j.tate.2004.04.009

Johnson, R. S., Mims-Cox, J. S., & Doyle-Nichols, A. (2010). *Developing portfolios in education: A guide to reflection, inquiry, and assessment* (2nd ed.). Los Angeles, CA: SAGE.

Kennedy, M. M. (1997). The connection between research and practice. *Educational Researcher, 26*(7), 4-12. doi:10.3102/0013189X026007004

Killion, J. P., & Todnem, G. R. (1991). A process for personal theory building. *Educational Leadership, 48*(6), 14-16.

Kleiman, S. (2004). Phenomenology: To wonder and search for meanings. *Nurse Researcher, 11*(4), 7-19.

Knight, J. (2007). *Instructional coaching: A partnership approach to improving instruction.* Thousand Oaks, CA: Corwin and NSDC.

Knowles, M. S. (1978). *The adult learner: A neglected species* (2nd ed.). Houston, TX: Gulf.

Larrivee, B. (2000). Transforming teaching practice: Becoming the critically reflective teacher. *Reflective Practice, 1*(3), 293-307. doi:10.1080/14623940020025561

Larrivee, B., & Cooper, J. M. (2006). *An educator's guide to teacher reflection.* Boston, MA: Houghton Mifflin.

Leeds, D. (2000). *The 7 powers of questions: Secrets to successful communication in life and at work.* New York, NY: Berkley.

Lindstrom, R. L. (1999, April). Being visual: The emerging visual enterprise. *Business Week,* Special Advertising Section.

Maloney, C., & Campbell-Evans, G. (2002). Using interactive journal writing as a strategy for professional growth. *Asia-Pacific Journal of Teacher Education, 30*(1), 39-50. doi:10.1080/13598660120114968

Marshall, S. P. (2006). *The power to transform: Leadership that brings learning and schooling to life.* San Francisco, CA: Jossey-Bass.

Marzano, R. J., Marzano, J. S., & Pickering, D. (2003). *Classroom management that works: Research-based strategies for every teacher.* Alexandria, VA: Association for Supervision and Curriculum Development.

McCutcheon, G. (1992). Facilitating teacher personal theorizing. In E. W. Ross, J. W. Cornett, & G. McCutcheon (Eds.), *Teacher personal theorizing: Connecting curriculum practice, theory, and research* (pp. 191-205). Albany, NY: State University of New York Press.

Mendler, A. N., & Association for Supervision and Curriculum Development. (2012). *When teaching gets tough: Smart ways to reclaim your game.* Alexandria, VA: ASCD.

Merleau-Ponty, M. (2002). *Phenomenology of perception* (C. Smith, Trans.). London, England: Routledge.

Mezirow, J. (1991). *Transformative dimensions of adult learning.* San Francisco, CA: Jossey-Bass.

Mills, G. E. (2003). *Action research: A guide for the teacher researcher* (2nd ed.). Upper Saddle River, NJ: Merrill/Prentice Hall.

Nye, B., Konstantopoulos, S., & Hedges, L. V. (2004). How large are teacher effects? *Educational Evaluation and Policy Analysis, 26*(3), 237-257. doi:10.3102/01623737026003237

O'Connell, T. S., & Dyment, J. E. (2011). The case of reflective journals: Is the jury still out? *Reflective Practice, 12*(1), 47-59.

Osterman, K. F., & Kottkamp, R. B. (1993). *Reflective practice for educators: Improving schooling through professional development.* Newbury Park, CA: Corwin.

Pelech, J., & Pieper, G. W. (2010). *The comprehensive handbook of constructivist teaching: From theory to practice.* Charlotte, NC: Information Age.

Pfeffer, J., & Sutton, R. I. (2000). *The knowing-doing gap: How smart companies turn knowledge into action.* Boston, MA: Harvard Business School Press.

Roe, M. F., & Stallman, A. C. (1994). A comparative study of dialogue and response journals. *Teaching and Teacher Education, 10*(6), 579-588.

Rogers, C. R. (1969). *Freedom to learn: A view of what education might become*. Columbus, OH: C. E. Merrill.

Ross, E. W., Cornett, J. W., & McCutcheon, G. (1992). Teacher personal theorizing and research on curriculum and teaching. In E. W. Ross, J. W. Cornett, & G. McCutcheon (Eds.), *Teacher personal theorizing: Connecting curriculum practice, theory, and research* (pp. 3-18). Albany, NY: State University of New York Press.

Sadala, M. L. A., & Adorno, R. D. C. F. (2002). Phenomenology as a method to investigate the experience lived: A perspective from Husserl and Merleau-Ponty's thought. *Journal of Advanced Nursing, 37*(3), 282-293. doi:10.1046/j.1365-2648.2002.02071.x.

Sammons, P., Day, C., Kington, A., Gu, Q., Stobart, G., & Smees, R. (2007). Exploring variations in teachers' work, lives and their effects on pupils: Key findings and implications from a longitudinal mixed-method study. *British Educational Research Journal, 33*(5), 681-701. doi:10.1080/01411920701582264

Schön, D. A. (1983). *The reflective practitioner: How professionals think in action*. New York, NY: Basic Books.

Seidman, I. (2006). *Interviewing as qualitative research: A guide for researchers in education and the social sciences* (3rd ed.). New York, NY: Teachers College Press.

Sisodia, R., Wolfe, D. B., & Sheth, J. N. (2007). *Firms of endearment: How world-class companies profit from passion and purpose*. Upper Saddle River, NJ: Wharton School.

SkyMark. (2011). *Force field analysis*. Retrieved from http://www.skymark.com/resources/tools/force_field_diagram.asp

Spalding, E., & Wilson, A. (2002). Demystifying reflection: A study of pedagogical strategies that encourage reflective journal writing. *The Teachers College Record, 104*(7), 1393-1421.

Sommers, W. A., Ghere, G. S., & Montie, J. (2008). Phenomenology. *Stanford Encyclopedia of Philosophy*. Retrieved from http://plato.standford.edu/entries/phenomenology

Tigelaar, D. E. H., Dolmans, D. H. J. M., De Grave, W. S., Wolfhagen, I. H. A. P., & van der Vleuten, C. P. M. (2006). Portfolio as a tool to stimulate teachers' reflections. *Medical Teacher, 28*(3), 277-282. doi:10.1080/01421590600607013

Tomal, D. R. (2010). *Action research for educators* (2nd ed.). Lanham, MD: Rowman & Littlefield Education.

U.S. Department of Education. (2003). *Meeting the highly qualified teachers challenge: The secretary's annual report on teacher quality*. Washington, DC: U.S. Department of Education, Office of Postsecondary Education.

Van Manen, M. (1977). Linking ways of knowing with ways of being practical. *Curriculum Inquiry, 6*(3), 205-228.

Watson, J. S., & Wilcox, S. (2000). Reading for understanding: Methods of reflecting on practice. *Reflective Practice, 1*(1), 57-67. doi:10.1080/14623940011554

Wong, F. K. Y., Kember, D., Chung, L. Y. F., & Yan, L. (1995). Assessing the level of student reflection from reflective journals. *Journal of Advanced Nursing, 22*(1), 48-57. doi:10.1111/1365-2648.ep8542692

Wright, S. P., Horn, S. P., & Sanders, W. L. (1997). Teacher and classroom context effects on student achievement: Implications for teacher evaluation. *Journal of Personnel Evaluation in Education, 11*(1), 57-67.

York-Barr, J., Sommers, W. A., Ghere, G. S., & Montie, J. (2001). *Reflective practice to improve schools: An action guide for educators.* Thousand Oaks, CA: Corwin Press.

ABOUT THE AUTHOR

Dr. James Pelech is an associate professor of education at Benedictine University, Lisle, Illinois. Holding an EdD in curriculum and social inquiry from National Louis University, Dr. Pelech moved to Benedictine University after teaching high school mathematics for 30 years. He was an officer in the United States Army Reserves for over 20 years, being activated for Operation Joint Endeavor, and retiring as a lieutenant colonel. Presently he lives in Joliet, Illinois with his wife Gwen, and son, Chris.

INDEX

CPSIA information can be obtained at www.ICGtesting.com
Printed in the USA
LVOW10s1246290713

345167LV00001B/13/P